Lant Carpenter

Sermons on Practical Subjects

Lant Carpenter

Sermons on Practical Subjects

ISBN/EAN: 9783743388611

Manufactured in Europe, USA, Canada, Australia, Japa

Cover: Foto ©Lupo / pixelio.de

Manufactured and distributed by brebook publishing software (www.brebook.com)

Lant Carpenter

Sermons on Practical Subjects

SERMONS

ON

PRACTICAL SUBJECTS,

(BY THE LATE)
Rev. LANT CARPENTER, LL.D.

ed.
EDITED BY

MARY CARPENTER

AUTHOR OF "OUR CONVICTS," "MORNING AND EVENING MEDITATIONS,"
"SIX MONTHS IN INDIA," &C., &C.

LONDON:
E. T. WHITFIELD, 178 STRAND, W.C.

1875.

ARROWSMITH, PRINTER, QUAY STREET, BRISTOL.

PREFACE.

The late Rev. Dr. Lant Carpenter was one of the Pastors of Lewins' Mead Chapel, Bristol, where he was highly esteemed for his ministry and his good works, both in his own congregation, and in the city generally. He also held a prominent position in the British Unitarian body, to which he belonged.

Shortly after his departure from this world in April, 1840, a volume of his sermons was prepared by his family for publication; this was edited by his eldest Son, Dr. William Benjamin Carpenter, the Physiologist, while his second Son, the Rev. Russell Lant Carpenter, prepared a Memoir of his Father. Both were published in a large octavo form, and were disposed of among friends by subscription. These volumes were not therefore extensively known.

Dr. W. B. Carpenter thus speaks in his Preface to the Sermons:—" No one who long attended on Dr. Carpenter's preaching, could avoid perceiving that he regarded it as his chief duty to impress his hearers with an operative sense of their Christian obligations ; and that he regarded all other objects as but secondary. Those who were best acquainted with the intellectual powers which he possessed, must have observed that, in his zealous devotement of these to his Master's service, he often restrained their exercise,—preferring the simplicity which could be understood by all, to those higher flights in which but a part of his audience could follow him. No wish has, therefore, been felt by his Family, to make this Selection convey an idea of his philosophic acumen, his critical learning, or his argumentative skill. They have rather desired to exhibit that to which he rendered these subservient,—his zeal and earnestness in the enforcement of the precepts of Christ, derived as they were from his deep conviction of their Divine authority,—the enlarged views he possessed of Christian duty, resulting from a faithful improvement of his religious experience,—and the warmth of that benevolence, which, springing perhaps from natural temperament, was expanded and invigorated by his steady aim to imitate his Great Master, and to carry on his work of love and mercy."

Sermons such as these, illustrated by the daily life of the preacher, must at all times be a useful help to those who desire to live in conformity with the Will of God, and in true development of the grand purposes of existence. They were greatly valued by all who had the privilege of coming under the influence of Dr. Lant

Carpenter's life and teachings, and the results of their teaching have been perceptible in the lives of those who received them. A period of thirty-five years since his lamented death has not diminished that sense of their excellence.

The present Editor, Dr. Lant Carpenter's eldest Daughter, feeling how largely she is indebted to her Father's influence and teachings, is desirous to extend them to the present generation, and has therefore selected the following Sermons from the original volume, with two not included in it. She hopes, by presenting them to the public in an inexpensive form, to make them generally useful. This volume will be accompanied by an abridgment of the Memoir, for which she is indebted chiefly to the Brother, who originally prepared it.

THE RED LODGE HOUSE,
   BRISTOL, *May* 3.

INDEX.

SERMON.		PAGE.
I.	God our Heavenly Father	1
II.	God the source of all	17
III.	"Dwelling in the light inaccessible."	27
IV.	Life and Immortality brought to light by the Gospel	38
V.	Open avowal of religious truth	51
VI.	The essential doctrines of the Gospel	64
VII.	"Think on these things"	74
VIII.	"We have corrupted no man"	96
IX.	Christian Patriotism	110
X.	The young exhorted to walk in the good old way	127
XI.	Ornaments and influence of the female sex	142
XII.	Hope in God	158
XIII.	The cloud not bigger than a man's hand	172
XIV.	The Christian's peace	182
XV.	"The will of the Lord be done"	195
XVI.	The will of God the best rule of duty	206

SERMON I.

GOD OUR HEAVENLY FATHER.

MATTHEW VII. 11.

IF YE, THEN, BEING EVIL, KNOW HOW TO GIVE GOOD GIFTS UNTO YOUR CHILDREN, HOW MUCH MORE SHALL YOUR FATHER WHICH IS IN HEAVEN GIVE GOOD THINGS TO THEM THAT ASK HIM.

HUMAN language necessarily fails when we are endeavouring to delineate the character and perfections of God. Nor is this wonderful. If the human imagination, in its most daring flights, cannot approach that light inaccessible in which He dwells;—if the human understanding, in its most cultivated state, and in its most perfect exercise, cannot find out the Almighty to perfection;—then the powers of language must fail, on a subject infinitely exceeding the utmost stretch of our intellectual powers. When we think and speak of the Most High, therefore, of His attributes and of His dispensations, it should be with humility and reverence, suited to the condition of dependent, frail, and erring children of mortality. He is in heaven, and we upon earth; and while dwelling with grateful delight, and filial confidence, on the goodness and paternal character of God, our pious affections should be refined and elevated by the sentiment which cannot but arise from the thoughtful contemplation of His almighty power, His unerring wisdom, His unbounded knowledge, His spotless holiness, and His moral administration.

It is one great advantage of the sacred Scriptures (and it is one among the many reasons which forcibly recommend the habitual perusal of them), that they represent the Supreme Being in various lights, and under various relations, and bring into view all the different ideas of His nature and character, by which our affections and conduct towards Him are to be regulated. We naturally feel disposed to dwell most upon those which best accord with our own dispositions, with the comprehension of our understandings, the leading principles of our religious belief, or with circumstances which, for the time, or habitually, operate upon our minds, and give a peculiar bias to our trains of thought and feeling. If we had nothing to check this tendency, we should speedily form very narrow and partial views of the Divine character. We should dwell upon the fearful power, and terrible majesty of God till we ceased to love Him; or upon His immensity and incomprehensibility, till we lost sight of His relation to ourselves; or upon his awful judgments and righteous justice, till we forgot His goodness and His grace; or perhaps upon His paternal love and pardoning mercy, till we imagined that His all-gracious compassion would not permit Him to punish; and deceive ourselves with the baneful and groundless expectation, that the weak fondness of the earthly parent would guide the Judge of all in the day of final retribution. But if we surrender our proud imaginations to the instructions of sacred truth, and found our views of the Divine character and dispensations upon them, and not upon our speculations, then we may reasonably hope to attain consistent, correct, and enlarged ideas of God and of his dealings towards mankind, such as will indeed be a light to our feet, and a lamp unto our path,—such as will make religion our delight as well as our duty, and will at the same time operate, with a holy influence, to produce watchfulness and steadfastness in our Christian course, and to make all the discipline of life conducive to our everlasting welfare.

Nevertheless, in the perusal of the sacred volume, we must faithfully employ that portion of understanding and information with which God hath blessed us. To pray for the wisdom which is profitable to direct, and not to use what we have, would prove us underserving of more. But if we dutifully use the light we have, we shall find more; and we shall not be often destitute as to any needful truth.

Our notions of the Divine character and dispensations have so great an influence on the whole tenor of our religious principles, that we ought to do all we can to form them correctly; and whether our attention is directed to those expressions respecting God, and His dealings to mankind, which were accommodated to the dark understandings and the gross conceptions of the children of Israel (and indeed the infancy of the human race in general), or to those more enlarged and refined ideas which we perceive in numerous parts of the Old Testament, and throughout the New; whether we think of God as the Sovereign Judge, or as the Shepherd of His people, as the all-powerful Creator, able to destroy with a word the universe He has formed, or as the constant friend and benefactor of His creatures;—we should be careful to direct, to restrain, or to exalt our conceptions and our feelings, by those fundamental principles which ought to be as a landmark in all our inquiries and meditations. We should have deeply impressed upon our understandings and our hearts that God is a spirit,—that He knoweth the inmost recesses of our hearts, and as the heavens are higher than the earth, so are His ways higher than our ways, and His thoughts than our thoughts; that His judgments must often be unsearchable by the finite understanding, yet that they are all guided by perfect wisdom and justice;—that with Him there is no variableness nor even the shadow of a change;—that He exercises His providential care towards every creature in every part of His unbounded universe;—and that He is love,—consummate, perfect, unbounded goodness, yet faithful to His threatenings as well as to His promises;—that He cannot be deceived, and will not be mocked, and will finally render unto every one according as his works have been. There are views of the Divine attributes fitted to raise the drooping heart, to strengthen the weak, to comfort the feeble-minded, to cheer the gloom of anxious care to encourage and animate the servant of God in the " patience of hope and the labour of love"; but there are also views fitted to strike terror into the guilty mind, and to alarm those who feel that they have not made God their portion and their friend.

Thus guarded, we cannot but be benefitted by the thoughtful contemplation of that endearing character, under which it has pleased God to represent Himself to His rational creatures, in order to encourage them in their obedience and in their trials, and to give to the pious heart the most cheering and impressive ideas of its duty. Indeed, if there be a spark of genuine virtue in the human heart, must not such thoughts cherish it? If there be any of the feelings of gratitude and love towards our Heavenly Preserver and Benefactor, must it not awaken, and enliven, and strengthen them, to reflect that such is His goodness, such His condescension to His weak and erring offspring, that, to encourage them in the way of holy obedience, to excite them to bear His image on their hearts, to support them under the trials of life, and to engage them to commit their souls unto Him in welldoing, He has been pleased to represent Himself to them as their *Father?*

The appellation is indeed a comprehensive one. In the words of one of our best devotional poets,

> "Parent, Protector, Guardian, Guide,
> Thou art each tender name in one."

And if we take care to exclude all debasing thoughts, derived from the weakness, the blind fondness, the narrow comprehension of the earthly parent, we may then safely indulge all those consoling, strengthening, and animating ideas which this relation suggests, which indeed are included in it. The appellation itself is cheering and encouraging; and I doubt not that it is in the experience of every one present, that when the heart is sinking under sorrow, or the apprehension of sorrow, when wounds have been inflicted which no human hand could heal, or when the child of God imagines that darkness and distress are in full prospect before him,— when all the offering has been the silent tear, and the emotions of humble pious submission,—if, in exercise of filial feeling he can say to Him who is ever present, "My God, my Father,"—the beamings of comfort and of hope penetrate the thick clouds of affliction, and show that the sun of divine mercy is still and for ever shining to diffuse rays of guidance and consolation.

I have, at times, endeavoured to illustrate the Paternal relation of God, by showing what is included in the earthly relation, when this is guided, not only by the natural feelings of a Parent, but also by sound views of human nature and human duty;—at the same time pointing out how much this view of the Divine character tends to cherish the disposition of filial service, to excite us to love our fellow men as children of the same Parent, to encourage us to cast our care upon Him who careth for us, and to lead to the exercise of implicit trust and dutiful resignation when He exercises us with affliction. At present, I wish to lead into other parts of the extensive field of contemplation.

The correspondence between the end and duty of the Paternal relation as exercised by the earthly parent, and that which God bears to His creatures, and especially to His rational creatures, is too obvious to require detailed consideration. It might be pleasing and profitable to point out the analogies at length; but my present object requires only a few brief remarks. God is our Father, as He is the source of being. He first gave life and all its vital powers to the wonderful fabric of our bodies. He is our Father, for He is our Preserver, Protector, and Benefactor. The streams of divine bounty flow indeed through human channels, and we sometimes forget the source from which all our blessings proceed; but on a moment's recollection we cannot but perceive, that

> "All the rich gifts that Nature brings,
> Are gifts descending from His Throne;"

that it is, in reality, His hand that feeds and clothes us, sustaining our bodily powers, enabling us to draw support and pleasure from the objects around us, and doing us good every day, every moment.

Thus far all His creatures are His children; but in a peculiar manner is He the Father of His rational creatures, the Father of our spirits. It is He who gives us those noble powers which distinguish us from the brutes that perish;—those powers which can trace out His being and attributes in the universe He hath formed;—by which He can communicate the plans of His providence;—by which we can meditate on things not seen;—by which we can penetrate into immeasurable fields of space; yet further, can look forward to an existence of unclouded light when time itself shall be no more. The Father of our spirits, it is He who formed us after His own image, who has made us capable of bearing the impress of His moral perfections, of becoming partakers of the Divine nature, and of rising in the scale of spiritual excellence from one degree of improvement to another, and to another in endless progression. Here we feel our conceptions of His Paternal character indeed exalted;—exalted above all the scenes of time and sense,—extended beyond the utmost limits of human comprehension. Ages, and ages, and ages, will pass away; but the noble principle which makes us indeed the children of God will know no decay;

and when ages and ages more have passed, still will know no change, except that which brings it nearer to the perfection of Him, who, however, must be for ever exalted above all finite excellence.

He is our Father, too, since in the methods of infinite wisdom, He is preparing His faithful and obedient children for this endless existence. All things will work together for good to those who love God. He maketh His sun to shine on the evil and on the good, and sendeth His rain on the just and on the unjust; and in *our* limited operations of Christian love, He requireth that we should imitate His unlimited and diffusive benevolence even to the unthankful and the evil. But we must in a peculiar manner regard him as the Father of those, who endeavour to be His children by humble pious obedience to His commandments; by grateful love for His obvious mercies, and by submissive resignation when these wear the form of afflictions. By discipline and by trial, by correction and by reward, He is training up our souls for holiness and happiness; and we are encouraged to believe that He orders all the events that befal His dutiful servants in that way which they themselves would desire, if they could divest themselves of all selfish partialities, and, with enlarged comprehension, consider all things in ther connections and consequences.

Since then, "God is the source" of all being, and of all power and capacities of body and mind, our constant Preserver and Benefactor, and our Guardian and our Guide;—since He is training us up for an immortal existence when this life is ended,—He surely is our Father.

Peculiar encouragement is afforded for these views in

the Gospel. It is seldom that our Lord speaks of God under any other appellation than that of *Father*. It is reasonable to conclude that this in part arose from the Divine words at his baptism, "This is my beloved Son, in whom I am well pleased"; yet it cannot be doubted that it proceeded in no small degree from the display, in his own work and commission, of the universal goodness and paternal love of God towards men. He not only spoke of God as *his Father*, and *the Father*, but often as *our Heavenly Father;* he reasons from the relation; he directs us to address Him as our Father in heaven; and presents to us the most solid ground for filial confidence, and for filial affection. We see in the Gospel a rich provision made by the Father of Spirits for the moral welfare of His children, by offers of pardoning mercy, and by sanctifying principles presented through His beloved Son. He has given a new and spiritual life to the humbled contrite sinner; and by the resurrection of Jesus from the dead, He has brought us again to a lively hope of an "inheritance, incorruptible, undefiled, and that fadeth not away." Surely he who hath Gospel views of the character and dispensations of the God and Father of our Lord Jesus, and amidst numerous imperfections and failings can, on Gospel conditions, hope that he is an object of the Divine favour, must feel an inspiring satisfaction and heartfelt peace,—such as the world knows not of, such as the world cannot give in its best delights, and such as the world cannot take away by its bitterest malignity,—when in the hour of solitary communion with his Maker, he can say with humble confidence, "This great and gracious Being is my God and my Father, He views me with a father's pity, and guides me with a father's care, He is my Father here, and He will be my Father through all eternity."

The paternal character of God affords a noble encouragement to the expression of pious affection in prayer and supplication with thanksgiving. Our Saviour expressly brings this into view in the words of my text. "If ye, then, being evil, know how to give good gifts unto your children, how much more will your Father that is in heaven give good things to them that ask Him." The philosophic inquirer who leaves the light of revelation, and has seen little and felt little of the workings of the human heart in connection with the exercise of prayer and devout communion with the Father of our spirits, is apt to find difficulties in the subject, which have in numerous instances checked the spirit of devotion, and caused that to be neglected which God hath made a grand and almost indispensable means of procuring the best of His blessings. Undoubtedly the great point is that we do His will; but what does His will respect?—Solely the external conduct? Assuredly not. It includes the regulation of the springs of conduct, without which there can be no religious obedience, or it will be weak, and limited, and unsteady. In a variety of instances the actions are the same in different individnals, while the qualities of heart from which they originate are utterly different from each other. In one case perhaps they may be alloyed with self in its less baneful form, or even debased by sordid and malignant passions;—in the other, perhaps, they have had their source in those noble principles, a sense of duty, Christian love, a pious disposition to obey God, and desire of His approbation.

Now a religious life (and let it never be forgotten that

a life without religion has no hope set before it in the Gospel) necessarily includes the dispositions and affections of the heart; and you may as well call him a benevolent man who makes the world his idol, who does good merely to gain its applause, and sacrifices at its shrine the simple principles of conscience and uprightness, and even the more enlarged directions of Christian love, as term that life religious in which God is little thought of, His presence little regarded, His will seldom expressly obeyed, His displeasure seldom expressly shunned, His favour but little the direct object of desire and motive of exertion, His mercies seldom traced to their source, His hand scarcely acknowledged even in affliction, in which in short the various affections of piety are not cherished and exercised. And how they can be duly cherished, and made stable actuating principles, without prayer, I know not. The acutest philosopher has never yet pointed out any adequate means; while man is the frail child of mortality, it never can be shown that we can do without prayer, unless we can do without piety.

How the Father of spirits operates upon the human mind, it may not be always easy to specify, nor is it necessary. By some means or other, directly or indirectly, He does operate; and I am fully satisfied that He has made sincere and humble adoration, thanksgiving, resignation, and supplication, in other words *prayer*, either mental or expressed in words, an essential instrument in obtaining that principle of piety, that Divine influence by which we are strengthened in the temptations of life, cheered in its sorrows, supported under its afflictions, encouraged in its anxieties, directed in its difficulties, aided and animated in its duties;—by which, in short, we are guided in the way of peace and security and holiness here, and prepared for that world where sorrow and solicitude and temptation will give place to complete excellence and happiness. It is not, perhaps, too much to say that it is impossible to walk with God, and to please Him with the obedience of our lives, without prayer in some or other of its forms. Seek, then, with full desire and purpose of heart, and ye shall find; let prayer be united with watchfulness and diligence in your Christian course, and it shall bring down the best of blessings.

The Paternal character of God affords the most encouraging hope to the penitent sinner. On this point again we are fully borne out by the representations of the Gospel. In the affecting parable well known to you under the title of the Prodigal Son, our Saviour has most distinctly brought into view the operation of a father's love in forgiving the sorrowing and contrite object of his displeasure. He wastes his substance in riotous living. But distress brings him to a sense of his sins, his folly, and his ingratitude; and he resolves to try what paternal compassion will work in his favour. He seeks not to be restored to his filial rank, but desires to be one of his hired servants. But his contrition is met with the indulgent impulse of paternal kindness; and he finds himself in the arms of mercy, as soon as his father sees the token of genuine and full repentance.

I do not believe that any human system can stand against the simple inferences from this impressive, and heart-reviving parable, where the disciple of Christ leaves himself to his Master's guidance. Paint the Almighty in all His terrors (and terrors indeed there are for the impenitent and disobedient), paint Him in all the awe of majesty and greatness, speak of His goodness and His justice, holiness, which will not allow Him to clear the guilty—humiliation and sorrow and alarm may seize the guilty heart; and it is well that they should, for often it is by these alone that the sinner can be made to see his danger and turn from his evil ways;—but let him see that there is no room for despair; let him know that the Lord God is merciful and gracious, long-suffering, forgiving iniquity, transgressions and sins: that even the holy men of old had declarations of His pardoning grace, and could affirm with pious confidence, "The broken and contrite heart, O God, Thou wilt not despise"; and that he who came upon the express errand of love and mercy, and who sealed the Covenant of grace with his blood, declared that there is joy in Heaven over one sinner that repenteth, and pronounced him an object of divine approbation, who with humble, contrite heart had smote upon his breast and said, "God be merciful to me a sinner."

The wisely affectionate parent, solicitous to prevent the contagion of evil among his children, to prevent the repetition of disobedience in the offender, will not from selfish weakness omit those corrective punishments which he sees necessary to support the authority, on the due exercise of which alone he can ground a solid hope of bringing them up in the nurture and admonition of the Lord. Sometimes, unable to penetrate into the dispositions of their hearts, and doubtful how far their professions of sorrow are produced alone by the fear of punishment (and not by the painful sense of his displeasure, and the wounds of conscience), he may justly hesitate in remitting the penalty of offence against filial and general duty;—but, when he sees good reason to believe that sorrow has arisen from right dispositions, and that it has done its work, in producing fear of disobedience in future, is he not ready, and more than ready, to clasp to his bosom the child whom he loves, even when his arm is lifted to correct? And can we suppose that God would make the parent able to entertain higher views of the paternal character than he will find realized in Him, whom he is taught to call upon as his Heavenly Father? Often the cries of penitence and the bitterest anguish, are but the temporary emotions produced by suffering, or by the dread of still greater suffering; often is that sorrow, which the human friend, with blind presumption, dares to pronounce a genuine repentance, and authoritatively to promise to it the Divine forgiveness, nothing but like the morning cloud or the early dew which soon passeth away; but if He that seeth not as man seeth, but looketh at the heart, discerns that godly sorrow which worketh a real and efficacious repentance, no doubt (I say no doubt because the Gospel declares it), He *is* ready to forgive, ready to exercise His paternal mercy.

Certainly it is a part of His all-wise dispensations, that repentance will not altogether remove the temporal evil that the sinner has brought upon his own head. This is necessary to maintain the sanctions of duty among those who cannot judge of the sincerity of repentance, and who need the warning of present punishment for sin. It is necessary even for the penitent himself; to excite him to watchfulness, to awaken his gratitude, and to promote more active exertion in the way of filial duty, more ready acquiescence in the dealings of God towards him. But sincere and effectual repentance must always *alleviate* the temporary effects of past transgressions and neglects of duty; it must cure or greatly lessen the spiritual evil which sin has wrought in the heart; it must restore peace to the wounded conscience; and, though the eye of the humble penitent must often be dimmed by the tear of contrition at the recollection of the past, still it can penetrate to the Throne of grace and mercy, and can look forward to the period, when, the ends of punishment having been fully answered, he shall experience no more the frailty and the sufferings of humanity.

Much more might be said, and if time permitted I might proceed to enlarge upon the encouragement and supports which the paternal character of God affords to the sincere Christian, in the various trials of life, and in the prospect of his last great change. But it is a subject on which it does the heart good to dwell, and we may have opportunities of again recurring to it. What a thought it is that He who is the Sovereign Lord of Heaven and earth, the Creator, the Preserver, the Governor of all things, makes the wants of every creature the object of His gracious care; and that, if we faithfully seek His favour, He will make all things work together for our good.

Go on, then, humble yet faithful disciple of Jesus, with tranquility and peace, in the way of providence in which thy Heavenly Father is leading thee, in the way of duty which He hath pointed out to thee, secure that it will conduct thee safely and well to regions of perfect light and happiness, where all darkness as to His dealings will be removed, and all sorrow for ever ended. In the hours of ease and prosperity, seek the favour of thy Heavenly Father, to employ thy talents to His glory, and to the best interest of those who are also His offspring, His children. In the hour of affliction, remember the hand from which it comes; glorify your Father by your pious submission and filial resignation, and by your wise improvement of His paternal chastisement. At all times aim to live as in His sight; maintain an habitual communion with Him in prayer and devout meditation; and then thou wilt be well prepared to meet all that He hath appointed for thee. If distrest, if perplexed, thou wilt never be forsaken. If earthly friends forsake thee, if thou art left to proceed on thy journey of life without the companions of thy course, in thy sorrow and thy joys, thou art not alone, for thy Father is with thee. He will be thy guide and thy guard, thy refuge and thy strength. In the dark valley of the shadow of death, His rod and His staff shall support and comfort thee. He will be thy never-failing portion, thy exceeding great reward.

May this, Brethren, be our blessed lot. May we be in truth the children of God, by living as the faithful disciples of Christ.—Amen.

SERMON II.

GOD THE SOURCE OF ALL.

ROMANS XI., 36.

FOR OF HIM, AND THROUGH HIM, AND TO HIM, ARE ALL THINGS; TO HIM BE GLORY FOR EVER, AMEN.

The Apostle, in the portion of his Epistle which he closes with these words, had been engaged in developing that appointment of Infinite Wisdom, by which the infatuation and unbelief of the Jewish nation had brought about the extension of the blessings of the New Covenant to all mankind. At the conclusion, he breaks out in the language of profound and cheering admiration, " O the depth of the riches both of the wisdom and knowledge of God; how unsearchable are His judgments and His ways past finding out." And then he (with an obvious reference to the sublime words of the prophet,* " Who hath directed the spirit of Jehovah, or being His counsellor hath taught Him?") continues, " For who hath known the mind of the Lord? or who hath been His counsellor? Or who hath first given to him, and it shall be recompensed unto him again?" That is,—Hath man rendered any service to His Maker, for which his bounties are only a requital? Certainly not. " For of Him, and through

* Isaiah xl, 13.

Him, and to Him, are all things; to Him be glory for ever, Amen."

In that most important branch of human knowledge which respects the character and government of God, there are some fundamental truths, which, when once we have acquired a reasonable certainty respecting the justness of them, we should employ as land-marks to guide us in all our speculations and inquiries, and from which we ought to allow no notions to lead us astray, derived from our partial observation of the events of life, or from detached portions of the Scriptures. The sublime and interesting truths contained in the comprehensive words of my text, are of this description. After we have once fixed upon our minds the conviction that those are truths, we should exercise that conviction; we should suspect our own judgments when they lead us to doubt with respect to them; we should pursue the application of them in the numerous instances in which this is clear, and consider the foundation of them in the perfections of the Divine nature. In short, we should cultivate faith and trust, humbly hoping that, if we attain the happiness of the blessed, our views will be more enlarged;—that we shall then be more able to see things in the light in which they are seen by the Infinite Being who ordereth all things in wisdom and goodness;—and that we shall then as clearly perceive that all being and all events, (even those which now appear most incomprehensible,) are contributing their part in the grand and comprehensive scheme of Providence, as we do now that all beings owe their existence and all their powers to Him, and depend upon His constantly operating energy, for the continuance of their existence, and for the support and exercise of those powers.

These, indeed, are truths which at once force our conviction, though they are too vast to be grasped in their full extent by the human understanding. The innumerable instances in which we can perceive the wise adaptation of means to ends, the skilful adjustment of parts to the purposes of the whole, the regularity and uniformity with which causes operate to produce effects, the wonders of the vegetable, and still more of the animal creation, and yet more the powers of our minds,—all operate to produce a conviction in the existence of a Supreme designing cause; which yields only to the influence of pride, or of that wickedness which shuts the understanding against truths which bring with them dismay and apprehension. The philosophic physician, Galen, became convinced of the being of a God, by the study of the human skeleton; and when we consider the astonishing mechanism by which the various functions of our bodies are effected, the numerous instruments of motion all admirably adapted to their respective purposes, the variety and delicacy of those organs by which the powers of life and sensation are supported, it seems impossible that any one capable of understanding the purposes and structure of the various parts of our frame, should doubt that it was formed by the wisdom and power of an intelligent First Cause. The researches and observations of the philosopher, whether directed to the structure and inhabitants of the earth, or to its situation and motions as one of an immense system of worlds, whether directed to the minutest, or to what we cannot but consider the grandest, displays of the Divine agency, alike contribute to increase the mass of proofs, that there must have been a designing Cause; and that He who created all things, and adapted all, and all their parts to their various purposes, must have been infinitely wise and powerful. In numberless instances, all that man has to do, is to observe and trace out the purposes of the various parts; and can it be supposed that these things could have come into existence by chance, which exercise the utmost skill of the human mind, and which reward its exertions by the perception of the most exquisite contrivance to answer the most benevolent ends? Even the little worm that crawleth on the ground is a sufficient proof of the existence of an intelligent and designing Cause. A patient observer of nature (M. LYONNET,) after the most accurate and long continued examination, discovered in the caterpillar which lives on the willow, no fewer than 4,000 muscles, which is nearly ten times as many as have been distinguished in the human body; all of them arranged in the most beautiful order, all subservient to the convenience of the animal, and all of them capable of motion, and producing motion at its will and direction. And He who formed this apparently insignificant animal with this wonderful mechanism, so formed innumerable worlds that they should move in their respective paths without confusion or interruption; and so formed the human being that, in addition to the astonishing and inimitable powers of life and sensation, he possesses an understanding capable of tracing out and admiring the Wisdom and Power by which all things were created, and affections which can be directed to the unseen Cause of all;—so formed him that he can know and love and obey his Maker.

Thus clear is it that there is a Great Being from whom are all things; and not less clear that by Him are all things, and that by Him the existence and powers of every being throughout His vast creation are continually maintained. That astonishing quality which we call life, is supported by the operation of a variety of causes, all of which derive their efficacy from His agency, which are in fact only instances of its operation. Were that agency withdrawn, the bond which unites the particles of matter with each other would be broken; the laws which regulate the motions of this world and all other worlds would be destroyed; the various properties of our bodies and of our minds would be annihilated; all would be without order, without life, without intelligence. We cannot but feel ourselves constantly and absolutely dependent upon Him for life and breath and all things; and those must indeed live without God in the world, who never observe and gratefully adore the guardianship of an invisible Hand, preserving them in life and preserving to them so many things which are calculated to make life a blessing,—who are never impressed, by the events which happen to them and around them, with the conviction, that all things continually depend on His sovereign will. Happy those who, by the various discipline to which He has seen fit to subject them, have learnt habitually to direct their thoughts to Him as their constant Friend and Benefactor,—to live as always in the presence of Him in whom we live and move and have our being,—to be grateful, obedient, and resigned.

And though so many and clear are our means of knowledge respecting the existence and attributes of the Most High, yet trust and resignation are qualities, the experience of which is often required in our passage through this state of trial. In what we commonly call the world of nature, it is not difficult to see, and generally to obtain a lively conviction, that all things are to Him,—that they all tend to the accomplishment of wise and benevolent purposes. But where man is much concerned, the immediate designing cause often conceals from our view the agency which in reality operates. Man often introduces apparent confusion, instead of that obvious order which is the inseparable attendant upon obedience to the known will of God; and in that confusion, our limited comprehensions seem scarcely able to perceive the ordinations of Him, who in reality guides, and guides all things well. Yet we have abundant grounds for the conviction, that, in the world of Providence, as well as in the world of nature, all beings and events are contributing their parts to the accomplishment of His wise and gracious purposes, that all is as He wills, and that His will is good. His judgments are indeed unsearchable, and His ways past finding out; but it is highly important for our own comfort, as well as for our entertaining right views as to the character and dispensations of God, that we should learn to acknowledge His superintending agency, learn to regard all events as making a part of His vast plan, and to entertain and cherish a firm and lively faith in the grand truth, that the whole and every part of that plan is so ordered by Infinite Wisdom and Power, that all must contribute to bring about the purposes of Infinite Goodness.

We must infer this truth from the known attributes of the Supreme Being. When we reflect upon the extent of the universe, as it comes within the limits of our own observation,—when we reflect that, vast as it is, there is no reasonable ground for doubt that it is only a small part of that indeed unbounded system which was at first formed, and is continually supported by Him,—when we consider how innumerable the tribes of living beings which the unaided sight can discover, and how small the number of these compared with that of the minute animals which are discovered by the assistance of the microscope, and how infinitely small the number of these compared with that of those which are the inhabitants of innumerable other worlds, and that all these must owe their existence to Him, and must continually depend upon Him for the support of that existence, and of their varied powers,— we cannot fail to perceive that His power must be unlimited (except indeed by natural impossibilities,)—and that it is, and must ever be, competent to execute whatever purposes Wisdom and Goodness may combine to form. And when we consider the evidence of that Wisdom by which this power has been directed, whether in its grandest displays of skill in the adjustment of the motions of the heavenly bodies, or in the wonderful adaptation of the various organs of the smallest insect to its wants and necessities,—when we attentively observe the numerous and admirable contrivances in the structure of our own frame, the suitableness of the parts to their respective purposes, and to the well-being of the whole,— when we consider how the functions requisite for life, for sensation, for thought, are accomplished, and by what delicate and wonderful mechanism,—when we call to mind that the same Wisdom which contrived the astonishing structure of the human frame, (which we cannot but admire the more we understand its organs and their uses,) formed the parts, and communicated and regulated the powers and properties, of all beings in every place throughout the unbounded universe,—the conclusion forces itself upon our minds, that the wisdom of God is indeed

Infinite. Our own noble powers become as nothing in the comparison; and we cannot but perceive that the most extensive grasp of human understanding, is competent only to trace out the proofs of Wisdom, which cannot be fully comprehended by any finite mind, but which has so constituted us, and probably all other intelligent beings, that we can gain from the things which are seen a conviction that the agency of that Infinite Power, by which all things rose into being, was directed in its operations by Infinite Knowledge.

We speak of Infinite Power and Wisdom; and from reflection on the works of God, and from the Revelation which He has been pleased to make of His character and government, we perceive that power and wisdom must be His attributes, and that they must be unlimited. But when we thoughtfully consider the extent of this truth, we cannot but be struck with amazement and awe; and while we adore Him who is thus possessed of Infinite Wisdom and Power, we cannot but rejoice that those attributes are guided by Benevolence equally unbounded. And when we have attained a firm belief in the declaration of the Gospel, that God is love,—corroborated and illustrated by the innumerable proofs of benevolence in His works and ways, mixed it is true with difficulties, which faith lessens but cannot entirely remove, but too decisive to allow of any other supposition than that God is good, and if good, Infinitely good,—when we have acquired this conviction, then our amazement and awe are blended with love and gratitude; and this Infinitely great and gracious Being can be viewed by us as our Father and our Friend.

When once the unlimited nature of the Divine Power

and knowledge is admitted, it follows as a necessary consequence, that all events are contributing to the accomplishment of His great designs. For, even supposing that God is only possessed of that degree of knowledge which is requisite for His being acquainted with every thing which takes place in every part of the universe, it cannot be supposed that He would permit any being to derange that plan, which He had appointed for the accomplishment of those ends which had been proposed by His benevolent Wisdom. But this becomes still more decided and clear, when we consider that Nature and Revelation concur in establishing the fore-knowledge of God;—that He must know all the effects which would be produced by the various powers with which he endowed His creatures;—that from all eternity every event and change throughout His whole creation has been ever present to His Infinite mind. Incomprehensible as the knowledge of the Deity is, and must ever be, to finite minds, yet all reflection on the other attributes of which He is possessed, lead to the conclusion that this also must be His. "If the entire frame of nature, now actually in being," (says ABERNETHY), "and the entire scheme of Providence which He is now carrying on, comprehending the whole series of events,—if these be the works of design, they must have been known before they began to be; and it is absurd, that powers wholly derived from and absolutely depending on a wise Author, for ends which He intended, should not be foreseen by Him, with all their exercises, and all their possible productions." Agreeably to this are the sublime declarations of the Prophet Isaiah, speaking in the name of the most High, (chap. xlvi. 9, 11,) "I am God and there is none else; I am God, and there is none like Me, from the beginning declaring the end, and from ancient times the things which are not yet done; saying, My counsel shall stand, and I will do all My pleasure; yea I have spoken it, I will also bring it to pass. I have purposed it, I will also do it."

When we have proceeded thus far, the conclusion immediately follows, that all events are but the gradual unfolding of that mighty scheme which through all eternity was present to His Infinite mind; and that all things must therefore have been so planned and arranged, that, however incomprehensible the means, they shall bring about the purposes of Almighty and All-wise benevolence; that of Him and by Him and to Him are all things.

SERMON III.

"DWELLING IN THE LIGHT INACCESSIBLE."

1 TIMOTHY, VI., 15, 16.

THE BLESSED AND ONLY POTENTATE, THE KING OF KINGS, AND LORD OF LORDS; WHO ONLY HATH IMMORTALITY; DWELLING IN THE LIGHT WHICH NO MAN CAN APPROACH UNTO; WHOM NO MAN HATH SEEN NOR CAN SEE; TO WHOM BE HONOUR AND POWER EVERLASTING: AMEN.

THERE are views of the Divine Being which are adapted to every valuable state of the human mind. Awe and reverence, wonder, love and gratitude, trust and resignation, all find abundant sources to excite and cherish them, in the contemplation of the being and attributes of the Most High. Is the heart attuned to delight and joy?—the riches of divine love present an inexhaustible fund for its most transporting emotions. Is it most in unison with those milder feelings, with which a sense of dependence is usually accompanied?—there is every thing to call them forth; the events which happen to us and around us, and the declarations of the gospel, all prove that in Him, and in Him only, we live and move and have our being. Do unexpected occurrences in life present peculiar degrees of happiness?—from Him proceedeth every good and perfect gift. Are we involved in deep distress?—He is the God of mercy and of consolation, He chasteneth His children but for their profit, and will make all things work together for good, to those who love Him. Does penitence heave the deep sigh at the recollection of past transgressions, and seek for some foundation on which to rest its hopes?—He is represented as the Lord God, merciful and gracious, willing to receive the repentant sinner, and desiring that all should return unto Him and live. Do the events of life appear involved in that mystery, which baffles the exertion of the strongest intellect fully to comprehend?—though clouds and darkness are round about Him, all His ways are mercy and truth; He will do that only which is right. Is the intellect in its full vigour, capable of the most profound investigation, and desirous to exercise its highest powers?—in the Divine perfections, works, and ways, there is a field of thought which ages would be insufficient to enable it fully to explore. Does the imagination expand its wings, and seek to soar beyond the objects of time and sense, to contemplate grandeur and awful sublimity?—He dwelleth in light inaccessible, He is infinitely great and wise and powerful, He is the King eternal, immortal, and invisible, everywhere present, everywhere and at all times exerting His agency, unlimited in all His excellences, the underived, self-existent Jehovah. If it stretch its daring flight to the utmost verge of what is known to us of the starry universe, and with the glance of thought (swifter even than the rays of light,) pass beyond the myriads, and myriads of myriads of suns and systems which philosophy has discovered, and take its station at the farthest spot to which human knowledge extends, it conceives ten thousand times ten thousand suns and systems, extending beyond each other in infinite progression, and is confounded when it contemplates the extent of that power and wisdom and goodness, by which all those worlds, with all their parts and properties, and all their inhabitants in all their diversities of structure and qualities, must originally have been created and still are preserved in existence; and it cannot but contemplate with sentiments of the profoundest reverence, and the deepest astonishment, that knowledge which is intimately acquainted with every event, throughout the unbounded universe, and that agency which is everywhere and constantly exerted to support the existence and functions of all its parts. In connection with the all-mighty, omniscient, eternal, everlasting, unchangeable, source of all being and perfection, the Creator and Preserver of all, the parent and friend of mankind, upon whose will we are constantly and absolutely dependent, and who (while He regulates the motions of worlds innumerable) supports the life and powers of every, even the most insignificant, thing that inhabits them,—in connection with this great and glorious Being, there is enough to exercise the noblest powers of the understanding, the most vigorous conceptions of the imagination, and the best affections of the heart, throughout the endless ages of eternity.

In the sublime representation to which those observations more particularly refer (that He who is the sole source of being and of power *dwelleth in light inaccessible*), the Apostle has (by some) been supposed to proceed upon the ideas prevalent among the Jews of the local residence of the Supreme Being; but I persuade myself that he had a much more elevated idea of Him who is a spirit, and who filleth heaven and earth with His presence; and that his words, even if founded upon these ideas, have no reference to corporeal light, but to that ineffable splendour and greatness, which attend all the Divine attributes, and surpass our most exalted conceptions,—to that inconceivable glory which surrounds all the perfections of the Most High, and renders them impenetrable to the eyes of the human understanding. I consider the Apostle as saying, that the nature of the Supreme Being is incomprehensible, and that His excellences are great and glorious beyond the grasp of every finite understanding.

I shall not at this time enter into the consideration of those mysteries which occasionally attend the proceedings of God towards His creatures. His judgments are indeed unsearchable, and His ways past finding out. We see but in part; and to grasp the all-perfect plans of Providence, we should be able to view them in all their causes, connexions, and consequences, as they are seen by Him, to whom the past, the future, and the present, are at all times and equally present. The greater the comprehension of the pious mind, the less its sight is interrupted by that gloom which sometimes veils the ways of Providence; and the more it has acquired of filial love and confidence, and dutiful submission, the less will what remains be felt. But it is well sometimes to penetrate beyond the darkness, in which to us the Most High appears, when viewed with an eye dimmed by earthly weakness and passions; and, at an humble distance, to contemplate the unspeakable glories of Him who dwelleth in light inaccessible.

His very *Existence* is glorious beyond all conception. All other beings are derived and dependent. Of the innumerable orders of the animal creation with which we are acquainted, from the little animalcule which is invisible to the unaided sight, to man, the noblest in the series, all obviously depend upon the Divine will for their very existence; and ascend in the scale of being high as we please, to the highest orders of intelligences of which we can form any conception, *derived existence and dependence* are felt to be their qualities; and we cannot rest in imagination till we arrive at the great I AM, self-existent, independent. Though He who formed the human mind, hath so constituted its powers, that, in their noblest exertions, they rise to Him, and, by the very nature of the mental fabric, are almost obliged to admit the existence of one Supreme intelligent agent, and thence to acknowledge (or else fall into the most glaring absurdities) that of necessity His existence must be absolutely underived, and of course absolutely independent,—yet the nature of His existence no finite being can be capable of fully comprehending. We can only say what it is not; what it is, is without a doubt incomprehensible to the highest orders of beings, most favoured with the brightest displays of the Divine glory. Even to them He dwells in light inaccessible.

And in like manner respecting the *Eternity* of the living God. We can add years to years, and call them ages; we can think of ages after ages (I do not mean that we can trace out in full succession the instants which compose them, but we can think and speak of them as we do of millions,—the imagination cannot form a conception of them in their parts, but can think of them as wholes); in the moments of solitary contemplation, we can imagine ages beyond ages, still continuing to pass and to have passed without a limit; and that is all. But this is not

Eternity. All we can say is what *it is not*; it is without beginning and without end. And this affords field enough for the utmost stretch of the human intellect. How easily the words pass over our tongues, and how easily the immediate meaning of them passes through the mind; but taken in their full comprehension, how vast and incomprehensible! Go as far backwards or forwards as we will, in the duration of the ever-living God, we feel that we are equally far from its commencement and termination; I should rather say, that we are equally far from any notion of a commencement or termination; that all we can think of it is, that it is without beginning and that it will have no end.

And throughout this eternal duration, the Divine Being is *unchangeable*. Here, too, the light in which He dwells is inaccessible. Like self-existence, this attribute is invisible, incomprehensible. We can form some, though an inadequate, conception of eternal duration; but the immutability of the Divine mind is beyond the utmost stretch of thought. We can *think* of *matter*, as lasting and changeless; we know that changes do take place in every thing we see around us; but we often see no change. The vast expanse of the ocean, though perpetually in motion, appears to the eye which contemplates it at a distance, unvarying in extent and surface; the towering mountain, or the solid rock, appear to undergo no change: and the heavenly luminaries which dispense light and heat to unnumbered worlds, present age after age, the same uniform appearance, and to human observation contain no seeds of destruction within themselves. But the moment we go into the world of *mind*, we find all continually changing. The succession of events, though not always dissimilar, is obviously different; and the progress of time is marked to us in various ways, by the changes which take place in the lives of others and in our own. But thought is ever changing. One idea, by the ever-active principle of association, brings on another, in endless and rapid succession. With all our boasted powers of comprehension, we cannot make two ideas at once the subject of our contemplation; and with our utmost cultivation of the abstractive faculty, we cannot detain a single idea in the view of the mind, so as to be in all respects the same one instant as the following. By self-culture we can by degrees learn to confine ourselves to the same subject and train of thought for a considerable length of time; but even the recurrence of the same ideas will be perpetually interrupted by others, resembling them perhaps in their character and effects, but not the same. How inconceivable the nature of Him with whom there is no variableness nor even the shadow of a change; to whom there is no succession of ideas; to whom everything that has ever been, or ever will be the object of thought, is now and at all times equally present. Language fails in our endeavours to express ourselves on such a subject; all we think and feel implies succession; and with our utmost efforts we seem incapable of forming any conception of the nature of that mind which is absolutely unchangeable. If any thing can give us a faint glimpse into the nature of this inconceivable perfection, it is,—

The unlimited extent of the Divine comprehension and knowledge. Here too the glory is inaccessible, but it is the glory of light; the other is rather the sublimity of obscurity. We feel certain that every event, every motion, every thought, of every being in this world, is fully known to Him whose knowledge is infinite; that the minutest as well as the greatest changes in the situation of all the parts of its material structure, and in the circumstances of all its animated inhabitants, are all at once perceived by Him. We extend our thoughts to the innumerable worlds which He hath framed; and feel alike certain that the same must be true of them and of their inhabitants. We trace in imagination the ages that are past; and we cannot but feel that all that has ever taken place throughout this unbounded universe must be in the view of the Divine mind, equally with that which is now present; that past and present are only notions of the human intellect, whose duration is succesive. And (though with more difficulty, because still more out of our own experience) we perceive, when we extend our view forwards, that everything future must always be alike present in the view of Him, to whom a thousand years are as one day, who from the beginning discerneth the end, whose counsel must stand, and who will do all His pleasure. This thought when we dwell upon it, fills us with the deepest emotions of wonder and astonishment: every change in the natural creation, and every event in the moral creation, throughout this and every other world, through all eternity, past, present, and to come, are all at once and for ever present to the infinite, unchangeable comprehension of the Most High. But it is inconsistent with no ideas which nature and revelation teach us of God. It follows directly from much that the Scriptures do teach us. It is itself a perfection. The mind revolts at the idea of limitation. It seems impossible to conceive that any limit can be set to the Divine comprehension and knowledge; and, with adoring awe, we receive as a sublime, though incomprehensible truth, that every motion, every thought, every change in the natural creation, and every event in the moral creation, throughout this and every other world, through all eternity, past, present, and to come, are all, at once, and for ever present to the infinite, unchangeable comprehension of the Most High.

I might now proceed to speak of the wonders of the Creator—how inconceivable the nature of creation, how immense the power of Him who spake and it was done, how infinite His wisdom, and how unbounded too His goodness: but perhaps we have thought sufficiently long on those incomprehensible subjects. What I have said is sufficient to show, that we have, in the attributes of the one Supreme Being, the noblest subjects of human contemplation, alike exalted and exalting, calculated to raise the mind above this world and its transitory concerns, and to lead it towards its home, where we shall know in greater and greater degrees, even as we are known.

Though the nature and perfections of the One Supreme are indeed unsearchable, let not this consideration lead us to admit any representations of Him which are inconsistent with what is known. Let us never forget the declarations of the faithful and true witness, that He alone is essentially and perfectly good, that He alone is all-wise, that He alone is all-powerful, that He is the only true God. Let us not forget the solemn declaration of Jehovah himself, "There is no God beside me." The highest of dependent beings, however exalted above all of which we have any conception, must still be infinitely below Him who is all-perfect, self-existent, underived, independent, and infinite in all His great and incomprehensible perfections. He is the blessed and only Potentate, He only hath immortality, He is the only wise God, incorruptible, unchangeable, everlasting, invisible, supremely great and supremely blessed; to Him alone religious worship is due; and His should be our highest, best affections of grateful reverence and love.

But, while thus engaged, let not our intellect become confused, and our faith waver. Though the existence and attributes of the Almighty are incomprehensible, yet are they real. If our conviction of His being and adorable perfection staggers, when we minutely contemplate the nature of that attribute by which He is at all times every where equally present, let us remember that it is enough for us,—enough to justify and excite our utmost exertions to be steadfast in the way of His commandments,—that He is acquainted with our thoughts, that He will be our Judge, and that He will render unto every one according to his works. If the imagination droops when it extends its glance to worlds beyond worlds and systems beyond systems, and contemplates all of them, and all their parts, and all their inhabitants, with all their varied powers and functions, and in all their mutual agencies and connections, as all depending upon His power,—let it rest in the assurance of him, who hath clearly revealed the most essential, perfections and purposes of his God and Father, that not a sparrow falleth to the ground without Him, and that even the hairs of our head are all numbered.

When we leave such sublime meditations, let us never forget that this great and glorious Being is, on the same authority, called *our* Father; that we are invited and encouraged to entertain towards Him (mixed with that reverence and awe which His perfections must ever inspire in the well-disposed mind) the warmest sentiments arising from the endearing relation in which we stand to Him; to view Him as our all-gracious and merciful Father, as ordering all things in wisdom and goodness, as the God of love, the Source of consolation, as everything that the mind can conceive of that which is excellent, adorable, and lovely. Such is the Being with whom we have to do; and shall we not love Him? shall we not adore Him? shall we not obey Him? By us may His will be done, as by those whom He hath favoured with brighter displays of His perfections, and a more perfect knowledge of His will; of Him, and by Him are all things; and to Him, the Lord Eternal, Immortal, and Invisible, the only God, be honour and glory for ever and ever.—Amen.

SERMON IV.

LIFE AND IMMORTALITY BROUGHT TO LIGHT BY THE GOSPEL.

2 TIMOTHY I., 10.

WHO HATH ABOLISHED DEATH, AND BROUGHT LIFE AND IMMORTALITY TO LIGHT THROUGH THE GOSPEL.

DEAR, then, to the noble aspiring mind must be that Gospel: dear, too, to the sons of sorrow! Must those "vast capacious powers" which "lie folded up in man" be bounded by the narrow limits of time? Must they cease to exist, often before the discipline to which the human soul is usually exposed has commenced? Often before it has brought them to maturity;—often when some pressure has prevented their expansion, or destroyed their vigour;—often when in their full energy of enlarged comprehension, of employment for the welfare of every one within their sphere of action? Must that mind which can glance through the vault of heaven, which can penetrate into the works of God, and discover the laws by which He directs His almighty operations, which can contemplate its own wondrous structure, can point its powers, and aspire after their unlimited improvement, which from the visible can infer the invisible, which can make an unseen, though not an unknown, Being the object of love, of veneration, of gratitude, of confidence,—must this noble principle sink into nothing, become as though it had never been?—and this, too, when its own effects still exist, when the plans which it formed or executed remain the everlasting monument of the being of a day, and excite the admiration, the respect, the gratitude, of those who have been the witnesses of its energies, of its virtue, and the objects of its benevolent exertions?

No, the creature of a day it cannot be. And yet, when the mind coolly contemplates the picture of reality, to what different conclusions it is often led, without some friendly hand to draw aside the veil which covers the recesses of the grave. All that displayed those powers ceases to present the delightful spectacle of their effects; and often, ere the lamp of life is extinguished, the bright flame of intellect, aye and of affection too, grows dim, and seems hovering round, waiting to expire only till the messenger of death closes the bodily eyes. The convictions of those who do not feel the force of the arguments by which the natural immortality of the soul has been defended, and, I apprehend, the convictions of many who do, would seldom stand against such appearances; still less against repeated impressions from the scenes which the sick chamber presents; were they not supported by that invaluable revelation which rises in the estimation of the soul, the more it is capable of appreciating its importance.

Besides, how many are there who pass their life without having had any opportunity of calculating the stretch of intellect, and who would perhaps be incapable of following it in its daring flights, or even of following the arguments which arise from the exalted nature of the mental powers; and those, too, among the classes of society to whom the doctrine of eternal life is of the greatest importance as a present solace.

But, it is urged, the ways of Providence would be involved in mystery, were there not to be a future life. Where would be the reward of suffering virtue,—where the retribution of triumphant vice? Where the refuge for the wretched,—where the consolation for the mourner? Hard must be the heart of him who would snatch away the staff which enables the child of affliction to support his weary way through the rough journey of life, who would shut the gate of future hope, when there was no longer the present hope to cheer. But while we have an anchor of the soul sure and steadfast, why rest this most important belief solely upon an argument, which, however powerful it may at times appear to cultivated understandings, will not prove the point, and which will often fail in its effect when the mind is less able to cope with difficulties, when yet it must need consolation? For if it be consistent with the goodness of an all-wise God to permit the appearances which now perplex, whence the proof that it is inconsistent with the same goodness, of the same all-wise God, to permit the perplexing appearances to continue? If they are unjust, where the pledge for a retribution from the same direction which now allows them? If they are just, where the ground to hope for a change? What we call evil, what we feel to be evil, certainly exists: if its existence is consistent with the goodness of God, what reason does it afford for the belief in a future life?—if inconsistent, all natural support of the doctrine from this source falls at once. Can it be proved that in any one case the sum of pleasing sensations and feelings is overbalanced by the sum of painful sensations and feelings?—can it be proved in any one case that the kindly affections have not on the whole an abundant reward in this life?—and, if so, where the ground for man to complain of his Maker should this life be all that he has to live? If there be a preponderance of pleasurable sensations and feelings among the sons of men,—still more, if it cannot be proved that this is otherwise with respect to any individual, we only diminish the difficulty, we do not remove it, by admitting a future life.

Let him who has this belief, however, cling to it as an invaluable possession. But I would gladly have him found his tenure upon the Charter of immortality. If God Himself had not informed us of a future life, I cannot see that it could reasonably be more than the object of hope; now, it is of confident expectation. It is of the first importance to render this doctrine efficacious, that the grounds on which it rests should be simple, easy to be comprehended by the mind, when its grasp is contracted by pain or debility or sorrow. It must not rest upon a long train of reasoning which perhaps at best is but specious, and which, however true, will lose its efficacy when the vigour which follows it is no more. It must not rest upon principles, which, (however readily the wish for a future life may countenance them, however readily the mind may imbibe them, when it is cheerful and active, when all appears gay and joyous,) would often seem full of doubt, when gloom depresses, when the mind distrusts the fairness of its deduction, and dares not admit what formerly gave it cheerful animation to believe. But let it rest principally on a fact which must be true unless God have worked a miracle to deceive His creatures,—let it be deemed one grand object of the message from God to man by Jesus,—and it will become as inwrought in the soul as the belief in Christianity. The appearances which confound will cease to affect the mind; for they cannot avail against an express declaration of the Word, the faithful Messenger of God. His resurrection proved that he was commissioned to reveal immortal life; and if he rose, then the hour must come when all that are in their graves shall hear his voice and come forth.

You may have seen, as I have, the feeling timid mind oppressed with the frequent survey of the decay of the human being, perceiving that all frequently appears extinct, incapable of discovering in the last scenes any thing that countenances the belief in a natural immortality of the soul, and daring not to lay down what ought to be the plan of Infinite benevolence; and you may also have witnessed the beam of grateful joy, when the true foundation of the Christian's hope and comfort was pointed out, when that connection was admitted, which is indisputably just, between the belief of immortal life and the resurrection of the Son of God, when the convictions which had been early implanted, but which derived all their vigour from a natural argument for a future life, which had therefore withered when exposed to the constant evidence of sense and experience, were again revived and invigorated by the cheering rays of Revelation.

If I am not solitary in these recollections, neither shall I be when I say that I receive with gratitude every confirmation of the revealed declarations of the Almighty which He has graciously afforded us from the more usual denotements of His will; but, inasmuch as assured hope, and confident expectation, in a point so momentous, are preferable to weak or wavering belief, so much do I see greater cause for gratitude, that the God and Father of our Lord Jesus, has, by the gracious message which *he* brought, dispelled all darkness, and, by the astonishing display of power in raising him from the dead, has left no room for hesitation, that his declarations are to be regarded as the words of the Father who sent him. Surely it requires but unbiassed reflection to admit in its full force the assertion of the Apostle, that Jesus hath brought life and immortality to light by his Gospel.

He says also, Jesus "hath abolished death." Were it not with the hope of rendering clearer words which seem to myself somewhat obscure, I would not change an expression to which I suppose the best hopes of almost every Christian are firmly bound. But Jesus has not *abolished* death; he came not to abolish it; he came not to make any change in the laws of Providence, but to bring them to light, to illustrate and confirm them, where they regard the duty and expectations of man. I believe that the words would be better translated, "who hath rendered death powerless." Indisputable is this assertion; for the Christian doctrine of a future life, changes the features of the gloomy tyrant, and disarms him of his power, in proportion as the disciple of Jesus obtains the victory over his own heart. Viewed with the light of Christianity the dark valley of the grave loses its gloom, for it is the passage to a new and eternal state of being; and that event which is regarded with dread as cutting off every source of tranquil happiness, as snapping every tie of tenderness, as breaking every project of benevolence, wears, under the Christian dispensation, an aspect in no degree tremendous to him who has fully imbibed the hopes of the Gospel. He regards it as the commencement of eternity, and as deriving its chief importance from that connection. If he can look forward with humble hope to the approbation of his final Judge, what should shock him? It is but a short night of quiet repose; and the morning of the resurrection will dawn on his view, close to the evening of life. And whether his habits of feeling have been so happy as to allow the moment of dissolution to lose all its horror, and all its pangs except the pang of temporary separation from the objects of affection, still death ceases to be regarded as annihilation, and the mind is relieved from the gloom without which annihilation cannot be viewed, except by the indifference and apathy of vice or false philosophy. Jesus has not destroyed death; but by his life-giving doctrine he hath rendered it powerless. As a mighty conqueror he himself rose from the tomb; and He who gave him the victory over death, will also by him give a like victory to his faithful followers.

Thus far we feel ourselves upon the surest ground; thus far the light of revelation guides us without any danger of error. And I believe we are upon sure grounds when we further affirm that there will be a general resurrection of all men;—a resurrection of eternal life to some, of condemnation to others. And if this be admitted, another conclusion seems inevitably to follow; which cannot in my opinion be overturned by passages of scripture which seem to lead to a different conclusion, but which can be fairly interpreted in consistency with this;—that the state of the dead is a state of unconscious existence,—that the interval between the moment of death and of the resurrection, is passed like the dreamless night of the wearied traveller, and like that too will appear as though it had never been. And to the individual, these moments will be as really in close succession as the beats of the clock; for it is too consistent with the nature of the mind to admit of a reasonable doubt, that the interval which we call moments may to some beings appear ages, while those which we call ages appear moments to others. All depends, as far as regards the individual, upon the succession of thought; and if that succession be altogether suspended, to him there is no time.

It is grateful, indeed, to the feelings of survivors, to believe that those whom we have lost are removed to a state of immediate bliss, that they are perhaps permitted to survey our conduct, and to watch over those whom they have loved, and for whom they " have wept and prayed in this vale of sin and suffering." And from those who have this belief, I have no wish to take it away. But few there are, who cannot read with placid pleasure, "there the weary are at rest;" and few, when they consider how much the mind which has not expanded into full comprehension grieves at the follies and vices of those who are objects of its knowledge, would wish to interpose such ideas to disturb that rest, still less to disturb a state of conscious bliss. It is grateful, too, to those who view with general resignation, but yet with momentary doubt, the various dispensations which remove from the scene of useful, of expanded benevolent exertion, those whose whole vigour was devoted to the cause of God and man, to think that the change is to them blissful; but to them the intervening interval is nothing, and the idea in no way removes the difficulty arising from suspension of usefulness to the world. Here, as in many other instances, we must trust where we cannot trace.

To the individual who has passed the bourn, it can make no difference what will be the nature of his resurrection. But such is not the case with the survivor. When we visit the graves of those who have walked in the path of holiness, if sorrow is not overwhelming, we feel a soothing emotion. They sleep as Jesus did; and God will bring them with him. They lie "under the smile of Heaven; and with the certainty of a resurrection to eternal life."

With respect to the nature of the happiness which will be conferred on those who have acted agreeably to the talents which they possess, and of the misery which will be the portion of those who have neglected to improve them, Christianity speaks only in general terms. And wisely;—for the attempt to particularize would have led to the adoption of language, which in many minds would have had no power, and which would have bounded the now unlimited expectation of all. As to those who have here departed from the path of holiness, I look forward to a period when, after age-lasting punishment, they shall all be brought into the fold of heaven. But the idea is more consoling to the good mind than it can be to the bad; for the representations of Scripture, the only guide which we can here follow with certainty, lead us necessarily to the inference, that those who have not here been led by the discipline of Providence into the way of righteousness, will undergo discipline in another state of being which will be tremendously awful; and which, in comparison with any present pain, will be infinitely agonizing in acuteness and duration. And, if we regard the state of bliss which Jesus hath brought to light, as a progressive one, then it indisputably follows that this punishment of the wicked will last through eternity; for through eternity they will be behind those in excellence and happiness, with whom they might have gone hand in hand in every stage of their progress.

It appears that we have abundant reason for the belief, that, whatever becomes of the more corruptible frame, all that constitutes the individual man, his habits of thought and of affection, will revive; and I know not how we can form a more exalted or more probable idea of a future state of immortal happiness, than by considering it as employed in the expansion and improvement, in the refinement and invigoration, of all that has here constituted real worth. The same beings whom we have seen quietly resigning their breath to Him who gave it, whom we have followed to the silent tomb, who sleep as Jesus did, and who now live only in the heart of friendship or gratitude or affection, and in the comprehensive mind of Him to whom a thousand years are as one day, will rise with all their capacities of enjoyment and improvement in their full vigour, with all those obstacles to enjoyment and improvement removed, which have here sometimes checked progress, and sometimes perhaps finally impeded it before the term of bodily health. Those who have decayed with age, or been worn out by the constant pressure of affliction, or by the rapid progress of disease, will rise with renovated life, with feelings no longer oppressed by suffering, or by dread of sin the worst of evils,—holding communion with the Father of Spirits, without those clogs which have interrupted their devotions, which made them sometimes fear that they were not the followers of God,—joining the heavenly society, composed of just men made perfect, and Jesus who led them to eternal life,—and spending their eternity in the blissful approbation of their Almighty Friend.

To this happy state may we all aspire; and, in the awful day of retribution, may we be admitted with those whom we have loved, to dwell with God for ever.

May we not go further and say,—living in the interchange of those more confined charities on which their general benevolence was founded, by which it was confirmed and invigorated, which here prompted to the noblest efforts, and constituted the greatest share of those feelings of joy which, arising from temporal objects, acknowledged a relationship with those which had their origin in God? It must be so. The soul which has here glowed with disinterested regard to the beings whom God had given to be led in the ways of holiness, which was willing to devote all its powers to their welfare, and to employ and improve them so as to lead them to live according to the great purposes of their being, has formed feelings and affections which individualize it, and which must revive when it awakes at the morning of the resurrection, and which will probably constitute one grand source of happiness in eternity. I know not why we should not admit a belief that those who are here guides and companions in the way of holiness, or who were pointed out by Providence as such, should not resume their situation in the abode of the righteous, and be in like manner occupied through eternity, without those impediments which here so often fill the mind with anxiety. Why should we hesitate to admit the belief that those who have founded their warmest affections towards man on the basis of religion, who have here studied the welfare of the small circle of friends, on principles which disinterestedness can acknowledge, will again enjoy those feelings when the short interruptions of the grave are over; that those who have travelled together in the journey of life, have shared each other's griefs, each other's joys, have aided each other in the way heavenward, will together share those joys which the gracious Father has promised to present continuance in well-doing, and heighten them by participation? I know not why we should doubt that the affection which sprung up first in the human soul, which grows with its growth, which has been cultivated with care when the more constant calls for it have ceased, which has been made the affection of duty, and risen when the affection of circumstances would have left little traces of its former existence, which has employed the efforts in smoothing the last stage of life, in supporting the trembling frame, and cheering the drooping spirit,—that this ennobling animating affection should not have its full share in the character, and constitute a full portion in the bliss of the inhabitant of Heaven, where it has done so in the inhabitant of earth.

The mind may sometimes dwell upon the expanded benevolence which Christianity holds out to our view,— and which, as constituting one grand branch of excellence, must form an essential part of the feelings of joy of those who attain the happiness of the good,—and may be led to suppose that all other more limited feelings will be swallowed up in this. But we need feel no difficulty. All that constitutes true worth of intellect and affection here, must make a part of the character in heaven; it is indisputable that we love all more as we love some more, if our affection be such as should survive the wreck of time; and—what puts the matter beyond all doubt in my mind—Jesus, whose benevolence was unbounded, and who had reached heights which it may acquire ages for his followers to gain, acknowledged and felt the character of friend and son.

Let it be our care, my fellow Christians, to improve the gift of God by Jesus; that at the great day of the resurrection, we may be found worthy to rejoin those whom we have loved and revered here, and dwell with them for ever.

SERMON V.

OPEN AVOWAL OF RELIGIOUS TRUTH.

MARK VIII., 38.

WHOEVER THEREFORE SHALL BE ASHAMED OF ME AND OF MY WORDS, IN THIS ADULTEROUS AND SINFUL GENERATION, OF HIM ALSO SHALL THE SON OF MAN BE ASHAMED, WHEN HE COMETH IN THE GLORY OF HIS FATHER, WITH THE HOLY ANGELS.

Since God hath appointed a day in which He will judge the world in righteousness, by that man whom He hath ordained, it cannot but be a matter of serious concern to every one who is heartily convinced of this most important truth, to ascertain the rules by which the decisions of that day will be guided. And, when he has ascertained them, it cannot be a matter of indifference to him, whether or not his conduct and dispositions so far agree with them, that he may hope to stand approved before his Lord.

Persons may, from habitual thoughtlessness or gaiety of heart, pass over the momentous truths of the Gospel, without being much affected by them. They may even make them the object of levity, alike injurious and criminal. But those who do seriously believe, that Jesus Christ spake the words of the Father who sent him, cannot think of these things, without at least a momentary impression. They may be too often driven from the heart, by the cares and pleasures of life; but when, (by any of those means which God has been graciously pleased to appoint, in the course of His moral government, to influence the hearts of His creatures,) those truths are brought home to the mind, they lead us—they can scarcely fail to lead us—to thought and reflection; and the solicitous inquiry is excited, whether we are steadily endeavouring to regulate our hearts and lives by the precepts of Jesus, and agreeably to his Divine example.

It is not perhaps one of the least advantages attending the usual religious services of the House of prayer, that those thoughts and reflections are often introduced by them into the mind,—not which suit our dispositions, or which, by defective views of duty, or by dwelling upon those worthy qualities which we really possess, flatter us into security as to our moral condition,—but which tend to enliven the conscience, to make it more susceptible and more powerful, to show us those duties in which we are negligent, to warn us of our errors and our dangers. In our private readings, we are too apt to slur over, or altogether neglect, those truths which would condemn us; but the representations of the pulpit, however little founded upon individual circumstances, must often be capable of individual application; and, where there is a right disposition, they will lead the hearer to try his own mental state by the principles of the Gospel, and thus correct, improve, and confirm it.

The connection of my text is briefly as follows. A few weeks previously to the crucifixion of our Lord, he went with his disciples into the more solitary parts of Galilee, and there inquired of them the opinion of the people concerning him, and also their own opinion. This led the ardent Peter to a distinct avowal of his conviction, that he was the Christ the Son of the living God. Jesus then immediately began to disclose to them the shame and sufferings which he was about to undergo; and afterwards, in the presence of the multitude, he inculcated self-denial, and pointed out the necessity of their being ready to give up everything at the call of duty. Attachment to his cause would, he knew, expose them to the greatest worldly privations and sufferings; and, with friendly wisdom, he endeavoured to prepare them for the trial, by furnishing them with those views which would lead them to regard worldly pains and losses as of comparatively little consequence, and worldly ease and pleasure as despicable, if to be purchased at the expense of their faithfulness to him. He brings into distinct prospect the transactions of that day, when, under the appointment of his God and Father, he will render unto every man according to his works; and, to counteract the influence of that false shame, which he knew would lead many to be faithless, and make the love of more wax cold, he shows them the unutterable disgrace and woe which must be the lot of those, who are here ashamed of him and of his words. "Whosoever shall be ashamed of me and my words, of him shall the Son of Man be ashamed, when he cometh in the glory of his Father with the holy Angels."

It is not difficult to perceive the force of our Saviour's words. They clearly and obviously point out at that desertion of him, or of his principles, which arises from the fear of censure and disgrace, or from the desire of obtaining the praise or good opinion of others. We are ashamed of Jesus and of his words, if, from loving the praise of men more than the praise of God, or fearing the displeasure of men more than the disapprobation of God, we deny or conceal our belief in Jesus as the Sent of God:—if, from these motives, we neglect those duties which he requires, or join in any practices which are inconsistent with the spirit of his religion:—if, from these motives, we countenance and encourage words or actions which tend to injure the Christian faith or practice of others:—or if from these motives we conceal, or directly disavow, those religious opinions which we feel convinced are Christian truth, or, by our words or actions, countenance and encourage those which we believe to be inconsistent with the doctrines of the Gospel, and to be in consequence directly or indirectly injurious to the Spiritual welfare of mankind.

I would not be understood to maintain that all these are equally sinful, and equally exposed to the fulfilment of the solemn censure passed by our Lord. He who has appointed him to judge the living and the dead, will doubtless enable him to award to every one in exact proportion to his deserts: and the punishment of the neglect or desertion of principle arising from false shame, cannot but depend in part upon the circumstances which tend to aggravate or lessen the sinfulness of such neglect or desertion, upon the degree of it, upon the continuance of it, upon the weakness or baseness of the motives which lead to it, &c. But I do not see how we can hesitate to admit, that every instance in which, from the influence of worldly honour or shame, we neglect or desert our Christian principles, (whether these directly or indirectly affect the practice,) is an instance in which we are ashamed of Jesus or his words; nor how, with the Christian rule of life as our guide, we can hope that such sinful shame will escape its proportionate punishment. We may qualify our conduct to ourselves; we may plead imaginary necessity as our excuse; or, in other ways, endeavour to lessen our culpability. But it cannot be too much remembered, in this as in every other branch of conduct, that we may tamper with our consciences, till we make them, for a time at least, speak what language we please. We cannot, however, alter the nature of right and wrong. We cannot much lower the standard of Christian duty. In the admirable words of Lindsey, " God does not want our sinful acts." It never can be *necessary* for us to do what duty forbids ; and we may satisfactorily indulge the fullest conviction, that, under the righteous government of our all-wise, all-gracious Father, it will always be best for us, and for others too, to do what we know to be His will.

Where a person is seriously affected by the truths of the Gospel, so as to be somewhat under the influence of religious principle, his regard to what he considers as Christian faith and practice, may be manifested, and will manifest itself, in various ways : and where that manifestation is in any degree voluntary, we call it a Christian profession. Whatever actions or course of conduct have a direct tendency to manifest his regard to religion, to the Christian religion, and to that one of the forms under which it appears, which he deems most accordant with the Scriptures, these form a part of his religious or Christian profession.—In this view, all peculiarities of dress, of language, or of manners, which are adopted from any religious views, are a part of a religious profession. In like manner, the regular discharge of the duties of family or social worship, is a part of a religious profession. The compliance with the ordinances of the Christian religion, is a part of a Christian profession. And, in like manner, uniting in any thing which tends to encourage and extend those principles of belief which he regards as Christian truth, is a part of his Christian profession.

The times are passed away, when the rack, the gibbet, and the flames, were employed to terrify the weak into a desertion of their religious profession, and to induce them to blaspheme that worthy name by which they were called. Worldly sufferings and disgrace are not now *openly* employed to make men ashamed of Jesus and his words. Yet there still are many circumstances of general occurrence, or which particularly affect individuals, which tend powerfully, and too often successfully, to weaken the attachment of Christian professors to that cause which they once viewed as the cause of truth and duty; to lead to compliances which their consciences, when pure and unbiassed by worldly motives, would have viewed as departures from the strict line of Christian sincerity and uprightness. In some instances, worldly advantages are unnecessarily, and therefore unjustly, (and at any rate injuriously,) made to depend upon the profession of certain religious sentiments: and the direct effect of this has been, in thousands of instances, to make men temporisers, if not hypocrites; and, in thousands more, to connect with religion desires and affections which have nothing to do with it, and which debase its value and its efficacy.

But the more general way in which a religious profession is hindered, weakened, or destroyed, is through the fear of censure or shame. The good opinion of those with whom we have intercourse, is generally so important to our comfort, and very frequently even to our usefulness, that we are reasonably affected by the desire of obtaining it, and of avoiding their censures: and where we are so happy as to mix principally with the truly worthy part of society, the desire of their approbation, and the apprehension of their disapprobation, are really valuable auxiliaries to the higher motives to the practice of duty. But not unfrequently, or rather very frequently, the feelings of honour and shame have a directly contrary effect. Except among the most depraved, the virtues which directly and obviously benefit society, are indeed approved of and the contrary vices reprobated: but among an extensive class, the gay, the frivolous, and the ambitious, (those whose chief pursuits are worldly pleasures and advantages,) all the higher virtues, all which naturally spring from religious principle, and partake of a religious character, and especially all strict attention to them, are very generally the object of contempt; and those who practise them must expect to be regarded by such persons as precise, formal, and even hypocritical. It requires considerable firmness of principle to maintain a religious profession in the circles of gaiety and fashion. The customs of those circles are little accordant with a due attention to the usual exercises of such a profession; and still less so, the too common dispositions of those who move in them. Totally unaccustomed to calculate the supreme importance of religious objects, the peculiarities which are connected with a religious profession excite their smiles; and by degrees they join in the silent sneer, or in the open ridicule, with which their companions may treat those who dare to wear the appearances of religion.

Among persons less thoughtless, and more depraved, every effort is often intentionally made, to make the professor of religion ashamed of his profession: and among those from whom better things might be hoped for, who have a general sense of duty and regard to it, there is too often a great disposition to shun, and even to treat with contempt and ridicule, all appearance of strict regard to religious duty. They are themselves afraid to be thought righteous over much, and they make others afraid of it too.

But where the desire of the world's good opinion, and the fear of worldly shame and censure, do not prevent or check a *general* religious profession, they often have this effect with respect to the *peculiarities* of religious profession. Christians still persecute each other, by their obloquy and their denunciations: and, to make a religious profession, agreeably to what a person believes to be religious truth, often requires considerable fortitude and steadiness of principle. The truly religious man, unless his mind be deplorably prejudiced, will always respect the conscientious profession of another, even where it widely differs from his own. But among the great bulk of those who make some profession of religion, it is too common to treat with contemptuous affectation of superiority, those who do not follow the multitude, who do not worship God in the most fashionable way; or most harshly to censure and revile those who leave what *they* think orthodoxy. From these causes, operating upon weak minds, upon persons who may possess some religious principle, but who are too desirous of standing well in the opinion of the world, forgetting that the love of the world is often at enmity with God,—such persons have often from these causes been known to desert a profession which they once might have honoured, ashamed to rank among those who have little worldly honour and respectability to confer, and who are (as they think) regarded so little by those who have the power and grandeur of the world in their hand. And numbers, from similar hopes and fears, have failed to avow their profession, and have carefully hidden their sentiments, or have at least neglected to employ those talents, by which what they really regarded as religious truth might be widely diffused.

And here I may add, that the neglect of the profession of what we believe to be Christian truth, really arising from motives of worldly fear or policy, is often countenanced and supported by an opinion, that all peculiarities of Christian belief are alike unimportant, and that, while men live as Christians, it is of no consequence what they believe. Without a doubt, Christian obedience is the grand point; and among all religious sects and parties, there are those who act up to, and adorn, their profession as Christians. But this opinion, to those who fairly consider it, without selfish prepossessions, must in my apprehension appear to be unfounded, as respects alike the nature of religious error, and the dispensations of the God of truth.—Where it finds a tendency to religious indifference, it gives countenance to it; and it often produces indifference where it does not find it. And, accordingly, it is a very prevalent maxim, among those who have not learnt to regard the knowledge and practice of the will of God, *as such*, as our grand concern as accountable beings.

Indifference has no real connection with candour;

though it often puts on its specious name. We may be too eager about points of faith; we may lay too much stress upon all adopting our own opinions as to Christian doctrine; but, where there is an indifference as to the peculiarities of religious belief, (except in very singular cases,) it will generally be found to spring from, or to cherish, great indifference as to religious principle and practice. And, because it has so direct and almost universal a connection with it, I would rather see some mixture of bigotry with our zeal, than a carelessness as to the truth or falsehood of those opinions which we regard as Christian doctrine. If God has been pleased to reveal His will and purposes to mankind, he who possesses an honest heartfelt desire to know and do His will, ought to think nothing unimportant which affects his own views, or those of others, as to that revelation: and, since indifference as to religious truth is so common among the indolent and lukewarm professors of religion, and still more openly among those who care but little for those things, those who have at heart obedience to the Divine will, should be on their guard against the chilling effects of that indifference; and, whatever obloquy they may subject themselves to, they should deem it as their bounden duty to endeavour, according to their abilities and opportunities, to know the truth as it is in Jesus, and to make their knowledge subservient to their progress in religious practice.

The desire of worldly honour, the dread of worldly shame, necessarily spring up in the human heart.—They are often useful aids of virtue: and, when well regulated, they are justifiable motives to action. But the circumstances of man as a social being, and the general processes of education, give them a degree of influence, which often fetters the mind to the objects of sense, and excludes the influence of the highest affections of our nature. The fear of singularity often operates so powerfully, that even the religious principle itself experiences its benumbing influence: and persons by whose light others might have been led into the paths of peace, conceal it, and thus, as far as the world around them is concerned, destroy its efficacy. This dread of singularity may arise from real humility, as well as from the fear of worldly shame. But the humble follower of Jesus should remember, that his master expects that his light should so shine, that others may be led to glorify our Heavenly Father; and those who habitually neglect acknowledged duties through false shame, should bear in mind, that of them Jesus has declared that he shall be ashamed when he cometh to judge the world.

Before I conclude, I would observe in the *first* place, that the prevalence of conduct which is inconsistent with a steady obedience to Jesus, and regard to his truths and precepts, will furnish no excuse for us in the last great day. Though the world around us presents degrees of wickedness which cannot but deeply affect the heart of the religious man,—though the attachment of many to Christ and his cause is weakened or destroyed by the abounding iniquity,—and though temporal motives too often tend to lead us all astray from the path of Christian duty,—yet, blessed be God, we have not the same difficulties to surmount with the first disciples. They did indeed live in a wicked and adulterous generation, when every worldly inducement was against their adherence to their Lord: and yet, even then, Jesus declared, that of those who should be ashamed of him and his words, he should be ashamed when he shall come in the glory of his Father.— We may think, and justly, that, in themselves considered, our departures from his cause are little in comparison with that complete desertion of it, by which some few at that time made shipwreck of faith and a good conscience; but let us also bear in mind, that neither can our temptations to be ashamed of him and his words, bear the slightest comparison with theirs.

Secondly,—The same prospects which Jesus held out to his immediate disciples are ours; and should be made our habitual motives to support our resolution under those smaller difficulties, perplexities, and privations, which may accompany a steady attachment to the cause of truth and duty. " Whoever shall confess me before men, I also will confess him before my Father that is in heaven: but whosoever shall deny me before men, I also will deny him before my Father that is in heaven."—As I before observed, he who was in all points tempted like as we are, will without a doubt be enabled exactly to appreciate the degree of worth or depravity of each one's character: and it does not become us to judge others;— to their own Master they must stand or fall. But for our own guidance, let us bear in mind, that a conscientious attachment to religion is indisputably our duty; and whenever, and in whatever way, we desert our religious profession, we so far expose ourselves to the awful censure of our Lord.

Let me add in the *third* and last place, that it is a delightful consideration, that every effort we make to bend our hearts and lives to the obedience of Christ, every sacrifice we make of selfish feelings and inclinations to the sacred calls of duty, every instance in which we proceed in our Christian course, in opposition to difficulties and discouragements, not only increases the firmness and purity of our religious affections and principles, and thus promotes our eternal welfare, but will of itself meet with the approbation of that Great Being, who is acquainted with every emotion of our souls, and contribute to give us that peace which the world cannot give or take away, which will smooth our present difficulties and exertions, and give tranquillity in nature's last conflict.—" Therefore my beloved brethren be ye steadfast, unmoveable, always abounding in the work of the Lord, knowing that your labour is not in vain in the Lord."

SERMON VI.

THE ESSENTIAL DOCTRINES OF THE GOSPEL.

1 PETER, III., 15, 16.

BUT SANCTIFY THE LORD GOD IN YOUR HEARTS; AND BE READY ALWAYS TO GIVE AN ANSWER TO EVERY MAN THAT ASKETH YOU A REASON OF THE HOPE THAT IS IN YOU, WITH MEEKNESS AND FEAR: HAVING A GOOD CONSCIENCE; THAT WHEREAS THEY SPEAK EVIL OF YOU AS OF EVIL DOERS, THEY MAY BE ASHAMED THAT FALSELY ACCUSE YOUR GOOD CONVERSATION IN CHRIST.

The object of the aged Apostle, in this excellent epistle was, to strengthen the faith of the Christians in Asia Minor; to direct them to the animating prospects of the Gospel; to cheer them under the persecutions which they were enduring for the cause of Christ; and to urge them to maintain that purity and propriety of conduct, which might put their enemies to shame, or at least might support their own hearts under their trials, and, while suffering according to the will of God, enable them to commit their souls to him in well-doing, as unto a faithful Creator.

The epistle abounds in weighty instruction and encouragement, suited not only to the peculiar circumstances of the first Christians, but to Christians of every age. It is full of evangelical motives and directions. It shows us our duty as disciples of Christ; and it encourages and urges us to activity and watchfulness in the Christian course, and to be holy in all manner of conversation.

To what hope the Apostle refers in the interesting and instructive passage which I have chosen for my text, must be obvious to every thoughtful reader of the epistle. " Blessed be the God and Father of our Lord Jesus Christ," (are his words near the beginning of it,) "who according to his abundant mercy, hath begotten us again, unto a lively hope, by the resurrection of Jesus Christ from the dead, to an inheritance incorruptible and undefiled, and that fadeth not away.' This hope was to be the anchor of their souls, sure and steadfast: and he directs them to it, in order to excite them to holy fear and resolution, as well as grateful joy. For this hope of final blessedness, they had indeed the best foundation; and he urges them to be always prepared to show that they had not embraced the Gospel without good reason; that while they sacrificed every thing on earth to the cause of that Saviour whom they loved, they could rejoice with joy unspeakable and full of glory, believing that when the chief Shepherd shall appear, they should receive a crown of glory which fadeth not away.

The original import of the text can scarcely be misunderstood; but I propose to accommodate it to the circumstances in which those stand, who, as Unitarian Christians, through adherence to what they deem the truth as it is in Jesus, are in these days so commonly spoken against. The directions in my text appear to me peculiarly applicable to our own case; and under the severest difficulties and trials which we may experience from obedience to what we think the dictates of Christian truth, we may imagine the aged Aopostle as saying to us—Fear not, neither be ye dismayed; but sanctify the Lord God in your hearts. Let him be your stay and your confidence. Let the fear of him be placed in opposition to the fear of the world. Entertain a cheerful confidence in his favour, while in the way of well-doing. Be assured that he will eventually make the truth of Christ prevail over all opposition. And while, in imitation of that Master who came into the world to bear witness to the truth, you do what in you lies to promote the diffusion of it, remember that God's time is best, and attempt not to hasten it by any means inconsistent with His will. Sanctify Him in your hearts; and let holy fear and filial love preserve you in the way of His commandments. Impressed with a deep sense of religious duty, seek for divine truth as a pearl of great price; and when you see reason for the serious conviction that you have found it, be ever ready, with mildness and with respect, to give to those who desire it, the grounds and reasons of your faith. Above all, exercise yourselves to have always a good conscience towards God and towards man; that by your Christian lives and conversation, you may put to shame the censures of prejudice or ill-will; and by the silent but impressive efficacy of example, promote that cause which, to the good man's mind, must be paramount to every other,—the cause of Christian truth and duty, the cause of Christ, the cause of God.

Under, I hope, the influence of the apostolic direction, I am desirous, this evening, to lay before you a statement of the essential doctrines of Unitarian Christianity.

I. We entertain, and desire to cherish, a steady and operative faith in God, as a Being all-wise, all-holy, all-powerful, and all-just—our Creator and Preserver, in Whom we live, and move, and have our being—of Whom, through Whom, and unto Whom are all things—the Creator and Preserver of all worlds and all beings, yet perfectly acquainted with the minutest event, and taking care of the meanest of His creatures—the Great Being with Whom we have to do, Who is the present witness of all our actions, to Whom all our thoughts and dispositions are fully known, and Who will one day render unto every man according as his works have been.

On this great and glorious Being, we know that we are constantly and absolutely dependent, for existence and for every blessing, in this life and in that which is to come; that it is by His grace we are what we are; that we are undeserving the least of His mercies; and that when we have done all, we are unprofitable servants. We know that it is our highest duty, with humility and godly fear, to obey His will, to seek His favour, to love Him with all our hearts, to submit with confiding resignation to His afflictive dispensations, to fear and honour and serve and glorify Him. We know that it is our highest privilege to trust in Him as the greatest, the wisest, and the best of all beings; and, in the way of well-doing, to cast all our cares upon Him, under a full conviction that He will make all things work together for good to those who love Him. We regard it as alike our privilege and our duty, to hold communion with the Father of our spirits by prayer, and by devout meditation on His works, and dealings, and word; to cherish a grateful sense of His mercies; and by supplication, with thanksgiving, to make known our wants unto God. We rejoice in the light which He hath afforded us of His will and purposes respecting mankind. We know that we are sinful creatures; we pretend to no merit of our own; and we look for the remission of our sins, and the salvation of our souls, in that way, and on those terms, according to which He has been pleased to offer them to us.

Respecting the nature of those terms, we leave many of our fellow-Christians, because we think that they leave the teachings of those who were themselves taught of God: but we trust that we, as well as they, are solicitous to know what God requireth at our hands: and that we are perfectly disposed to accept of the offer of salvation, in whatever way, and on whatever terms, He hath seen fit to make it. To know what these are, however, we cannot bow to human authority; but regard it as our duty to seek for them, with seriousness, humility, and diligence, in the Holy Scriptures. And this leads me to observe,

II. That we regard the Scriptures of the Old and New Testament, as containing a faithful record of divine revelation; and, in particular, that the New Testament contains a faithful record of all-important revelation which God made to mankind by Jesus Christ. We regard the Scriptures as the sole authoritative rule of faith and duty; we know that they are able to make us wise unto salvation; we know that they will guide us to life everlasting; and it is our earnest desire and endeavour to ascertain what they teach, and what they enjoin. In doing this, we are desirous to avail ourselves of all the light which learned and eminent men have thrown upon the sacred writings; to know what the Apostles and Evangelists really wrote, and to ascertain as nearly as we can what they meant. When difficulties occur, we compare scripture with scripture; and believing that revealed truth cannot be inconsistent with itself, we hold, that whatever, through the imperfection of human language, is obscure, or of doubtful meaning, ought, in reason and common sense, to be interpreted by the clear and express declarations of the Scriptures in other parts. But we are convinced that the grand truths of religion are written in the sacred page in characters so legible that the wayfaring man need not err therein; and we doubt not that whoever comes to the Scriptures, with an honest desire to know and to do the will of God, will be led by them into all needful truth,—that they will be a lamp unto his feet and a light unto his path. In interpreting the Scriptures, we cannot bow to the decisions of any human authority; but in reverence for divine revelation, and for the Scriptures as containing that revelation, as containing the word of God, we wish to yield to none of our fellow-Christians. We regard the glorious Gospel of the ever-blessed God, as His unspeakable gift to the children of men. And,

III. We agree with our fellow-Christians much more than many of them are aware, respecting the character and offices of our Lord Jesus Christ. We believe in his divine authority, in the divinity of his doctrines and his mission,—that he was the Christ, the Son of the living God. We seek for no other foundation on which to rest our hopes here and hereafter, than that which is laid, which is Jesus Christ. We believe that God manifested himself in and by him; that he is the image of the invisible God,—since in and by him the glorious perfections of God were eminently displayed, and His wisdom, goodness, and mercy manifested to mankind. We know that he set us a perfect example of sinless excellence; and we contemplate his character with admiring veneration.—

We believe that he gave himself for us to redeem us from all iniquity; that he executed the purposes of grace and mercy for which he came into the world, at the expense of every worldly privation and sacrifice; that to fulfil those purposes he voluntarily submitted unto death, even the death of the cross; and that being made perfect through suffering, he became the author of an eternal salvation to all that obey him. And thus viewing him, as, under God, our Saviour and Redeemer,—as bearing all, and enduring all, in obedience to the will of God, and laying down his life for our sakes,—we, too, glory in the cross of Christ, and feel that he is entitled to the warmest gratitude and love.

But we follow our Saviour from Calvary to the throne of God—from that period when he was despised and rejected of men, to his exaltation. We see the stone which the builders refused, become the head of the corner; that same Jesus who was crucified, raised, by the mighty power of God, exalted by His right hand to be a Prince and a Saviour, appointed to be Lord of the dead and of the living, to raise the dead, and to judge the world. And viewing him as our Lord and Master, as appointed by God to be our spiritual Sovereign and our final Judge, we feel that he is entitled to our reverence, our faith, and our submissive obedience. It is our earnest desire to bear his image in our hearts, to imbibe and cherish his spirit, to walk in his steps, to keep his commandments, and to abide in his love. We earnestly desire to be his, living and dying, at the last great day, and for ever. And when we hear the denunciations of bigotry, or the assertions of ignorance, against us, we feel disposed to adopt the language of the Apostle, and say, "If any man trust to himself that he is Christ's, let him of himself think this again, that as he is Christ's, even so are we Christ's."

Those who are already convinced that these great principles are the doctrine of the Gospel, let me urge to act up to their profession and privileges. You have, my friends, an animating conviction that your cause is the cause of God and Christ; and you look forward with satisfaction to the period, (which the attributes of the God of truth, and the express declarations of prophecy, encourage you to expect,) when "Jehovah shall be king over the whole earth;" when "Jehovah shall be one and his name one;" when all men shall bow the knee to the God and Father of our Lord Jesus Christ, and every tongue shall confess that " Jesus Christ is Lord, to the glory of God even the Father." Let it be your endeavour, as you have opportunity, to contribute to this great end, and to diffuse the knowledge and practice of the Gospel.

You have clear and unembarrassing ideas of the great Object of worship: you have no ground for doubt and uncertainty to which Person you shall address your prayers and praises and the adoration of the heart. Let your worship of God even the Father, in public and in private, in the house of God, in your families, in your religious solitude, be ever animated with the pure spirit of devotion; let the offering be the language of the heart; let it be offered in spirit and in truth: and let your devotion be transferred into your lives, earnestly desiring to glorify God in all you do through Christ Jesus.

You have views of the Father of mercies, the God of all consolation, which exclude all servile fear, where the heart is devoted to His service. You can think of Him as perfectly good and merciful, as love itself; and while you forget not that He will render unto every man according to his works, and therefore pass the time of your sojourning here in godly fear and holy watchfulness, let your study of the ways and of the word of God lead you to higher and higher degrees of love and gratitude to Him. Endeavour to love Him, according to the direction of your Lord and Master, with all your heart; and, in imitation of him whom you love and desire to obey, to do the will of your Heavenly Father and to finish His work, resigning yourselves and all your concerns, for time and for eternity, unreservedly into His hands, with a full confidence that He will then make all things work together for your good.

Free from the limited ideas which many entertain respecting the bond of Christian fellowship, and the terms of divine favour, show forth, in a greater degree, the genuine dispositions of the Gospel of love and peace. Be ever ready to unite with them in the common objects of Christian love; and convince them that you are not here destitute of the spirit of him who hath commanded us to love one another.

In fine, since you believe that you have attained clear ideas of Christian duty and Christian obligation, since you know that you must each, on the last great day, bear your own burden, and that then your condition must be determined by your dispositions and conduct in this life, let it be your earnest, steady aim, to abstain from the pollutions of the world, and to perfect holiness in the fear of God. In sincere and humble piety, in reverence for the name, the word, and the worship of Almighty God, in the love and imitation of Christ Jesus, in benevolence, and uprightness, and truth, and love, in moderation and

Christian sobriety, let your light so shine before men, that others seeing your good works may be led to glorify your Father who is in Heaven. Whatever you do, in word or in deed, do all in the name of the Lord Jesus Christ. And in the path of Christian duty, may you possess the supports and comforts of the Gospel; in every trial and perplexity may it guide you in the way of Christian truth and uprightness; and may the peace of God which passeth all understanding keep your hearts and minds through Christ Jesus. Amen.

SERMON VII.

"THINK ON THESE THINGS."

PHILIPPIANS IV., 8.

FINALLY, BRETHREN, WHATSOEVER THINGS ARE TRUE, WHATSOEVER THINGS ARE HONEST, WHATSOEVER THINGS ARE JUST, WHATSOEVER THINGS ARE PURE, WHATSOEVER THINGS ARE LOVELY, WHATSOEVER THINGS ARE OF GOOD REPORT;—IF THERE BE ANY VIRTUE, AND IF THERE BE ANY PRAISE, THINK ON THESE THINGS.

I PERSUADE myself that there are few amongst you, who do not at once feel that this is a noble and comprehensive passage. The epistle from which it is taken, was written by Paul, aged and in bonds, to a body of Christians for whom he obviously felt a tender interest; and who on various occasions manifested a grateful attachment to him, by contributing, as they had the power, to alleviate his affliction. It is written with the cordial feeling of one who knew that there were hearts to receive, and heads to comprehend, those enlarged views of duty, and those elevating sentiments of piety, and those glorious prospects of Christian faith, which had long become the settled and matured principles of his own mind; and which, in various ways, manifest themselves in all his writings.

The general import of the passage itself is at once obvious. The diffuseness of the translation somewhat weakens the emphatic character of the original; but there is only one of the expressions employed which does not convey its import; I mean, whatsoever things are *honest*. In the common signification of the word *honest*, that is included in *just;* the original word means *venerable*, or *respectable*, that which deserves respect or reverence for its excellence and dignity. *Honest* formerly had nearly the same meaning as *honourable*, and in that sense our translators obviously employed it.

Those who are acquainted, as we all should be, with the invaluable writings of the Apostle, cannot be ignorant that he always presents the various branches of duty in their connection; he viewed them as all arising from godliness as the root, and as deriving, from this ennobling principle, that which gives them their greatest vigour and most salutary influence; and he viewed them too, in their connection with faith in Christ, as all comprehended in the Christian's obligation to love, imitate, and obey him, who came forth from God to guide us in the way of peace and blessedness.—This is the case in the present instance. He had just directed to the best and truest refuge in the solicitudes and trials of life: he exhorts to prayer and supplication with thanksgiving, and the laying open of all the desires of the heart before Him to whom all hearts are open, all desires known: he declares the blessed effects of habitual piety, in that peace which the world cannot give or take away, and which, by its tranquillising, strengthening influence, would promote perserving steadfastness in Christian duty; and then in the words of my text, he points out the virtues which this will lead us to exercise,—*truth and uprightness ;—purity and love ;*—and he does not omit the *graces* of the Christian character, but directs the attention of his brethren in Christ, to all that accords with true dignity and honour, all that deserves approbation, all that is *of good report*. It was his *happiness* to be enabled to enforce all, by a reference (suitable and impressive from Paul the aged, the prisoner of Christ, their friend and spiritual father,) to his own example,— " Those things which ye have both learned and received, and heard and seen in me, do, and the God of peace shall be with you."

Finally brethren, whatsoever things are true, whatsoever venerable, whatsoever just, whatsoever pure, whatsoever lovely, whatsoever of good report,—if there be any virtue, if any praise,—think on these things—think on them with the reflection of the understanding, and the earnest and effectual desires of the heart.

It is often desirable to dwell on *particular virtues* of the Christian character, to show their importance and their direction, to excite to the practice of them, or to aid in strengthening their influence ; but it is also well sometimes to take more connected views of duty, that we may feel more sensibly, at what we have to aim, and that, while cherishing one grace or excellence of the gospel, we may not forget that there is no disposition in which duty has no concern, no branch of conduct in which its principles have no direction or control. If the young (whether in age or in moral culture) would lay such things seriously to heart, they would soon experience how true it is, that like the sun in the world of nature, Christian principle sheds its influence over the whole course of life; that where it has taken up its abode, it is continually guiding, stimulating, restraining, strengthening or refining; and that nothing is more salutary in preserving from the worst of evils, and in urging on in the noblest work, (that of duty and self-discipline), than the habitual tendency to refer our conduct and dispositions to the standard of the gospel under the influence of its motives. This will not unfrequently lead to humbling and even painful reflections; but in humility there is peace, and such pain may yield a godly sorrow unto repentance; and conscience will become more prompt and correct; and our moral judgment more clear and decided; —our way will be more secure, our views of Christian obligation will enlarge, our spirits will be more chastened; —and if Christian faith fixes its abode in the heart, without losing the smallest portion of cheerfulness, or of vigour in the laudable engagements of life, we shall find that there is an internal principle which will preserve us from the evils that corrode the joys of the heart, and which will guide us with steadiness in the paths of righteousness.

It was my principal object in selecting the words of my text for our present meditation, to illustrate them a little and show their extent of application. I would say to those who are setting out in life,—take them as your maxim and your law. They will conduct you securely and honourably. I would say to all, think on these things, frequently, earnestly, seriously and effectually, and the God of peace shall be with you.

I. Then, let *truth* be the object of your thoughts, and of your earnest pursuit. Whatsoever things are *true*, those esteem and practice. The virtues have a close alliance one with another. Truth in words has an intimate connection with justice in action. Uprightness includes both. The upright man must abhor falsehood. He will not only avoid those flagrant violations of truth, which all, who have any moral principle, must condemn (where they are the base means at attaining ends as base, selfish gain, or malignant revenge,—where they are employed to blacken the reputation of others, or to further the objects of villany), but he will not hold as guiltless the falsehood prompted by the fear of censure or disgrace, by the love of distinction, by vanity or cowardice, by the foolish desire to practice on the credulity of others in order to glory over it, or by any view to selfish convenience or interest or the avoiding of personal evils, nor even by those advantages to which benevolence itself may appear to direct ;—certain that in every case the way of uprightness alone is the way of safety, and that the good of God's creatures will always be best secured by obedience to His will. To maintain the course of simplicity and godly sincerity, often requires prudence and fortitude; but these are necessary, not only in every department of duty, but in the more important engagements of life; and it is one of the innumerable ways in which godliness has the promise of the *life that now is*, that it leads to the culture of those views which impart prudence, and affords the noblest supports to fortitude, in difficulty and danger. Let simple aims, let moral caution be acquired, and the love of duty will guide in perplexities in which *he* must be embarrassed, and perhaps fall, who is double-minded, and therefore unstable in all his ways. He who has fixed in his heart a serious respect to God as his constant witness, and a solemn sense of accountableness, and under the influence of these great principles is resolved, with the divine blessing, that conscience shall guide him and not the world's law,—the fear of God, and not the fear of man,—will be prompt to perceive, and firm to follow, and quick to regain the course of duty, while others waver and are lost.

But the Apostle's words respect not merely veracity, or the duty of truth, but truth in opinion; and the love of truth in this sense affords a noble guidance. Where the influence and importance of truth are duly appreciated, and the mind is accustomed to desire it, to seek after it—and, where it respects duty and moral sentiment, to carry it into practice—it easily perceives the injuriousness and folly of those paradoxes and sophistries by which the young are so often misled, through the persuasion of their own misguided inclinations. Without this love of truth as duty's friend, they soon learn to regard as uncertain, truths alike certain and momentous: the dictates of conscience are tampered with; the maxims of the men of the world are set up in opposition to them; the strict morality of the Christian is deemed unsuitable to the state of society; fixed principles which would guide with honour and with peace, are relinquished for the guidance of the more dazzling and daring assertions which appeal to interest or passion or self-indulgence; the duties of piety are neglected;—by degrees God is well-nigh forgotten, and faith in unseen realities ceases to have its controlling influence—present pursuits and pleasures absorb the thoughts and desires—and this world is *practically* considered as *all*.—And yet, as the glorious luminary of heaven shines with undiminished brilliancy, whether or not he is discerned through the dense mist or in the lurid tempest, truth remains in all its lustre, though the mind may be surrounded with the sophistry of vice, or involved in the tempest of passion; and even then God hath not left himself without witness, or man without direction. The chart and the compass remain to guide. The gospel of Christ clearly traces the duties and the dangers of man, and conscience directs which course to pursue, and which to shun. Some truths should be regarded by the mind as fixed principles, and nothing should induce us to relinquish them, or to maintain them with wavering purpose. —"Thou God seest me,"—and, "After death the judgment,"—have this indubitable character. And even if that blessed gospel which affords the best support to faith in God and things unseen, should cease to have, as it once had, the lively conviction of the heart, yet amid all the fluctuations of the understanding, these truths should remain unshaken; and if ever we feel our faith in them wavering, or perceive the world keeping them out of sight, let conscience take the alarm, and let us shun the broad path which leadeth to destruction. We cannot, by any speculations or reasonings, shun the omniscient eye of God; nor, by any exertion of human intellect, can we prevent our hearing the voice of him who will call us forth from the tomb to life or condemnation. Let these solemn truths, then, be habitually thought of,—thought of as truths,—as certainties; and if the mind be placed under their influence, it will have truth in view more than the dazzling novelties of speculation. If these should be pursued in order to sharpen and invigorate the intellect, it will always be with subserviency to higher objects, and with the caution of one who thinks nothing in the efforts of the human mind so venerable as truth, nothing so deserving of respect and reverence. No wonder, then, that the Apostle followed his exhortation to the earnest pursuit and practice of truth by directing the attention of his friends to

II. Whatsoever things are *venerable*; whatsoever deserves respect or reverence. If the mind is trained to consider things in the relation they bear to the great ends of life, its sentiments of respect will commonly be well directed. It will be able to look further than the glare of the world—to times and circumstances where, if a brighter lustre is not shed, all is gloom and darkness. Yet even in the dignities and honours of the world (dependent as these are for their influence on the happiness of him who attains them, on the way in which he gains and employs them,) there is usually much which makes them lawful and even laudable objects of human desire, if not appreciated too highly. Never are they truly respectable to the individual if they are to be gained only by the sacrifice of principle; never, if when attained they are to be employed only for the purposes of selfish ambition and interest. Let them be sought, if God has given us talents and opportunity to seek them, as what *may* add to the happiness, but will certainly call for increased watchfulness, expand the circle of duty, and give greater responsibilities; and, if attained, let them be held as a trust, as affording increased power of usefulness, and more commanding influence on human welfare. Thus viewed, the eager grasping of the worldly desires may be lessened, but higher and nobler purposes and energies will be called into action; worthy objects will be sought after, with a different but not less effective aim;—if they are not attained, disappointment will not sour the heart, or throw a gloom over the course of life; and, if attained, God will

G

not be forgotten in the honours and homage of the world around us, nor will the glory hereafter to be revealed be concealed by the pomp and lustre of the present.

But heights of wealth or power, or intellectual eminence, like those to which the aspiring mind, much influenced by the estimate of the world, will sometimes glance, are within the reach of but few; they do not give the highest dignity; they often mislead from that which is truly respectable,—that which, whether found in youth or in age, in the elevated walks of life, or in the abodes of the humblest poverty, gives real dignity. When the mind, led to serious thought by the solicitudes or sorrows of life, views things in the light in which they should habitually be viewed by beings designed for eternity,—what is it that then appears most deserving of respect, most truly eminent? Is it not the possession of those virtues which adorn the character, which give it grace and moral dignity? The eminence on which the world places a person *may* give him honour, but these *must*. Spiritual excellence is true greatness. And when death has terminated the earthly career, and the splendours of the world cease to affect the mind in its estimate of those who were surrounded by them, how completely do we feel, that the faithful, serious, humble discharge of duty, the mild graces of the Christian, the union of the upright and the lovely, the love of truth and of purity, shed over the tomb a lustre on which the mind can rest with full satisfaction; and make the memory cherished, and embalm it with an admiring respect, which talent, or rank, or wealth, unaccompanied with moral worth, and undirected to the welfare of others, can never command.

Whatsoever, then, is truly respectable, seriously consider, and earnestly pursue. Seek for dignity in truth, and uprightness, and purity, and benevolence. Let the welfare of others (in the wider or narrower circle, according to your sphere of influence,) be an object of your faithful aims. Let it influence you in your pursuit of knowledge, in your usual employments; and allow it to curb the promptings of the mere selfish desires. Let the most venerable of all objects, religion, and the sublime exertions of self-control to which it points, the subjugation of worldly interests or passions, be habitually in your contemplation. Think on these things, till your hearts glow within you, and your desires are up-raised, and your imagination carries you to the presence of Him in whose sight nothing is venerable but that which will be venerable for ever. And then will you be well prepared for the insinuations and the sneers of those whose intellects, however gigantic in the fields of science or literature, are unable to comprehend the dignity of the soul, or to appreciate that which raises in the well-trained heart sentiments of admiring veneration. Think on these things, till your moral sentiments become elevated, till your standard is high-raised, and then your mind will be prepared to estimate objects in their true light; and you will see, as you cannot otherwise see, how degrading is vice, how full of shame are the pollutions of the world.

You cannot then expect to find what is truly dignified, except in company with justice and with purity; and to these objects of the apostolic recommendation I now proceed.

III. Whatsoever things are *just*, contemplate and pursue. Justice, the best moral writers among the ancient heathens pronounced to be the sovereign of all the virtues; and certainly it is itself of essential moment in the character, and the best ally of all the higher virtues. It consists in rendering to all their dues; it leaves out of view our own narrow interests, where they interfere with the equitable claims of others. It requires that we estimate these by other tests than those which *self* directs; that we be not too tenacious of our supposed rights; that we faithfully consider the rights of others, and that we consider those rights as extending not only to their pecuniary interests, but to their reputation and their peace. If we carefully think of this department of duty, so as to perceive its extent and importance, we shall find its influence presenting itself in all the various relations of life, curbing the excesses of self-love, restraining and regulating our words and our actions, and even our dispositions where they affect others.

As the intercourses of society and the relations of property extend, so must the claims of justice become more comprehensive and extensive, and the necessity of it more obvious; and yet, these very circumstances also present greater temptations to depart from its strict principles. More interests interfere; personal welfare seems (to the narrow mind) more independent of the welfare of others, or even more in opposition to it; the plainest directions of justice become capable (as it *seems)* of modification and reserve; so that he who has no firm principle of uprightness within, or is destitute of the noblest support,—the fear of the Lord and desire to do His will,—often loses that discrimination of right and wrong, and that love and appreciation of justice in opposition to selfish interests, which once influenced his mind. This is most perhaps to be apprehended where other distinctions than those of truth and uprightness are to be the guide and ground of decision; and where the claims of justice are often baffled or lost sight of, in the short-sighted rules and forms of human invention.

Against all these perversions of the understanding and moral principle must we carefully guard. Truth and uprightness are *not* empty names; nor ought they ever to lose their influence over our conduct. Let us keep our standard of estimation *upright;* if that be made to bend to us, we shall never raise our minds to that noble sense of uprightness, that love of it, and attachment to it, which, firmly gained, will be like a rock to support us, among the ebbs and flows of popular opinion, and the boisterous waves of interest. There are often critical moments in a person's life, in which his moral character is at stake. One departure from duty commonly leads to another, and the only safety is, in *being always* upright; and the only way to be always upright, is to regard uprightness as a duty of indispensable obligation, not only to man, but in the sight of God; to guard against selfish purposes; to exercise ourselves to *have always* a conscience void of offence; to judge of things by the rules by which we must one day be judged; and to every temptation to depart from the plain path of integrity, to present a prompt and unhesitating reply, "I cannot do this great wickedness and sin against God."

IV. Whatever things are *pure* are next urged upon our solicitous consideration and exercise. The Apostle's writings come too directly from the heart, and have too little the characters of logical refinement, to allow us to infer much from the arrangement of these several virtues; but though his noble eloquence, dictated by exalted thoughts, often soars above all the restraints of art, yet it is almost impossible to follow him critically, without perceiving the proofs of that high intellectual training which he must have received in the schools of philosophy at Tarsus, and afterwards at the feet of Gamaliel; and what could have been more proper, had he studied the arrangement, than the place which he has assigned to each of these qualities, which he thus presents in combination? Purity is a powerful ally to uprightness. Whatever tends to fix the soul on selfish desires, and to increase the exorbitancy of self-love, must be the enemy to justice, and prepare for encroachment on the rights of others. As the claims of self are magnified, the claims of others either appear to be lessened, or at least cease to have the same influence in checking the efficacy of those dispositions which lead us to slight the duties of justice. Profligate licentious habits continually lead to injustice. They do it in part by occasioning expenses which the circumstances of the individual cannot bear; thus presenting direct temptations to fraud and dishonesty and violations of confidence; and by degrees leading to great and fearful breaches of social duty, often such as expose to the severest animadversions of the law. But they do it still more, and even with greater moral injury, by lowering the tone of moral principle,—by weakening the sense of duty,—by leading to slight, and then to throw off, the restraints of religion and conscience,—by making God neglected,—and by excluding from sight as much as possible, those solemn realities, which, even if with an unobserved influence, *should* operate continually on the mind, and preserve from sinning against Him who ever knoweth the way that we take.

How much those baneful pursuits, which so often have given them the name of *pleasures*, are continually defeating the best hopes of friends, and interfering with the fairest prospects, how often they either prematurely cut off from life, and (where they do not) inevitably treasure up for advancing years decay of body, disease and wretchedness, and restless fearful distress of mind,—is known to all who observe the course of the abandoned, and even of those who have not resolution enough to shun the haunts of the wicked, though they do not altogether ose the sense of religion in their hearts.

But it is not direct and open immorality alone which will be shunned by those who seek the blessings of purity. This high quality has its seat in the heart, and where it rules there it will guard the thoughts, and urge to discipline them; and it will make the retired actions such, that the eye which ever seeth, will see in the most secluded recesses nothing which can wound the conscience, nothing to stain the fair robe of virtue. It is a fearful truth that outward decorum may be preserved, and yet the heart be debased; and therefore they who aspire to the blessedness of the pure in heart, will early and perseveringly endeavour so to cultivate such a command over their trains of thought and imagination, that obtrusive thoughts and imaginations, if they enter, may be banished by such as leave no sting or stain behind them—such as religion can approve, or at least pass by without condemnation. This mental command is powerfully assisted by the steady fulfilment of the regular employments of a person's station in life; and it is also powerfully exercised by the steady pursuit of useful knowledge; while at the same time *this* furnishes the mind with subjects which invigorate and elevate, and often lead on to Him who is the source of all light and knowledge; and thus, as in numberless other ways, knowledge is the friend of virtue.

Whatsoever things are *pure*, study and pursue. To comply with this precept of heavenly wisdom, that true delicacy and modesty must be cherished, which will shrink from offensive language, and from unhallowed thoughts. Those recesses which the eye of man doth not penetrate, it will remember are constantly open to Him who knoweth the imaginations of the thoughts; and the secret ejaculation, and the stated prayer of the heart seeking after God, will be found, where united with watchfulness, to be the most effectual preservations against the pollutions of sin. That watchfulness is in no way inconsistent with the cheerful intercourses of sociality, and with other innocent recreations; but it requires temperance in all allowed indulgences, in sleep, in diet, and in mere amusement, and the avoidance of indolent gratification, and of dissipating pursuits, and of whatever tends to enfeeble the mind, and render it indisposed to the proper engagements of one's calling and relations in life.

It may not be deemed unsuitable to observe that the maternal friend, influenced by Christian principle, will sedulously endeavour to direct her daughters in the cultivation of that " true delicacy which consists in purity of sentiment;"—not the delicacy of mere ignorance, but the purity of imagination and desire. They will guard the plant of modesty with assiduous care; they will lead to the observance of that decent personal reserve, which is so closely connected with real refinement of heart; and they will prevent unrestrained intercourse with companions of suspicious delicacy. Without encouraging that fastidiousness, which is at best but a suspicious friend of purity, they will not be afraid of being thought fastidious; and bearing in mind the requirement, "whatever things are pure," they will think more of wisdom and duty than of fashion, and never allow genuine modesty to be without support, or the want of it to be without censure, or at least obvious disapprobation. Happy will it be for the interests of virtue, when the female sex not only cherish modesty and purity in their own breasts (which happily is no uncommon case), but make it obvious that virtuous conduct is of more weight with them than the brilliancy of wit, or the fascinations of fashion;—and when (in those early trainings of the youthful heart, which so much devolve upon them, and in that influence in riper years which they can perhaps best exercise), they lead the other sex to cultivate a respect for moral purity, and a love of it, and that "self-control" which was declared to be "wisdom's root" by one, who through the want of it blighted his fairest prospects, and sunk into an untimely grave.

I know not how the serious intelligent young can fix upon a surer guidance than this noble passage. While dwelling upon it, one can scarcely avoid perceiving that close connection of the different branches of virtue which it recommends, all springing from the great root of religious principle. I adverted to the connection between justice and purity;—see how this is connected with the love of truth, and particularly of the greatest of truth. In an admirable discourse of the late Dr. Lindsay, on a kindred subject, the eloquent preacher observes, "To a virtuous man what idea is so delightful, as that of living under the protection, of moving under the guidance, of approaching to the resemblance, of being destined to the fuller knowledge and more perfect enjoyment of, unchangeable and everlasting goodness? A heart that has no evil propensities to gratify, can have no temptation to listen to the vain sophisms of pride and sensuality, by which the wicked delude themselves into unbelief in order to escape the terrors of a guilty conscience. It is the interest of such a heart to hear the testimony of nature within, and the assurance of scripture from without, that the eyes of the Lord are in every place, beholding the evil and the good. For what solace can such a heart feel equal to that which arises from filial confidence, from humble hope, from the assurance that, after having experienced the joys of devotion here, as far as is consistent with the ends of a probationary state, it shall ultimately become a nobler and fitter habitation for the spirit of God."

That purity of heart which the Gospel requires extends also to all those base desires and malignant passions which lead in their habitual tendency to the contraction of moral guilt. "The heart that harbours pride, or covetousness, or envy, or revenge, though it may never have known the power of the grosser appetites, is not therefore entitled to the praise of being pure." And though the Apostle here I believe refers peculiarly to purity in the common sense of the term, yet how obviously is it connected with the next requirement:—

V. That we study and practise *whatever things are lovely*,—whatever in our dispositions and in our external conduct is calculated to render a person the object of love or complacent esteem.—Whatever causes an exorbitant attention to self, whatever cherishes our own high thoughts of ourselves, and leads to seek inordinately our own comfort or reputation, whatever excludes from sight considerations which are fitted to introduce a kindly attention to the feelings and reputation of others,—tends to interfere with this direction of the Apostle; and hence it is among other reasons that impurity has so powerful a tendency to destroy the higher degrees of benevolent affection.

The customs of the world, introducing an artificial politeness, often throw a cloak over those dispositions which affect the happiness of those who are more exposed to their influence,—for instance, in the domestic circle; even such restraint is valuable, and makes the intercourses of society more accordant with the spirit of the gospel; and not unfrequently those who have little restraint from a sense of duty, acquire the captivating manners with which one would wish virtue to be always accompanied. But where a sense of duty does not enter the heart, the self-willedness, the love of gratification, the self-indulgence, which are all cherished by a regardlessness of the virtues of Christian sobriety, all tend to make the lovely in the external deportment (whether real or assumed,) but little the object of attention, in those intercourses where, in a thousand nameless ways, we are able to promote the peace and comfort of those around us. On the other hand, when Christian principle has a powerful influence in the heart, it leads us to dwell upon and to cultivate not only the essential virtues of the moral character,—truth and uprightness and temperance and purity,—but to pursue and practice those qualities which adorn and which influence the hearts of others; not only those which give stability and consistency to the character, but those which make it lovely.

The requirements of the Gospel are clear and express on this point, and it does not leave it to ourselves whether or not we will exercise these graces of the heart. It makes the kindly affections a part of duty. It places us under an obligation, as the disciples of him who pleased not himself, to be kindly affectioned one to another; to mind not merely our own, but the things of others also, in honour preferring one another; to restrain the emotions of anger and envy, and uncharitableness. It requires us to be compassionate, merciful, forgiving, and courteous; not rendering evil for evil, or railing for railing; not willingly offending, or being easily offended; and exercising patience and forbearance under real injuries. It is at once obvious that, in proportion as the spirit of the Gospel brings forth these fruits in the heart and in the life, must the direction of the Apostle be fulfilled. These are what are truly lovely. The exterior may sometimes be assumed; and, by the restraint imposed on the expression of wrong feelings, the feelings themselves may often be checked, suspended in their exercise, and even replaced by kindlier emotions. But the true way, the most lasting and most effectual way, is that which is pre-eminently the gospel principle, to subdue and regulate the heart itself. The Christian will endeavour to subdue arrogance and vain glory, contempt of others and a fond conceit of himself; he must bring down his high thoughts of himself to a just level; and, by curbing every excess of self-love, and entirely repressing all its inordinate promptings, and by benevolent consideration of the peace and comfort of others, and by real desires to promote the happiness of all connected with him, he must (not in order to be thought amiable but to *be* so,) pursue steadily those things which are lovely. It is necessary that in this he never lose sight of those virtues which deserve respect. We must not be men-pleasers, if conscience would be wounded;—we must not aim to gratify at the expense of truth and sincerity;—nor pamper pride or malignant passions in order to please;—nor, in order to conciliate affection and regard, say peace where there is no peace;—we must never sacrifice principle, in order to obtain love. But wherever it is only self that we are to give up,—unreasonable desires, uncharitable judgments, hasty unkind censure, and the expression of arrogance and bitterness,—there let us think on whatever things are lovely.

VI. And lastly, whatever things are of *good report*, deserve our thoughts and our endeavours, from a regard, not only to the love and to the happiness of others, but also to our own usefulness and happiness. The estimation in which others hold us, is of great moment as affecting our ability to do them good and to gain their aid in doing good to others; it affects their conduct towards us in various ways, and must necessarily have great influence on our comfort and welfare. It is well, it is necessary, to be able to deliberate and to act, without influence from the sentiments of others (even of the wise and good,) respecting our conduct; there are often occasions when the heart must rise above the opinions of the thoughtless and the dissipated; there are occasions when the good opinion of the world around us must not even be thought of, but only the straightforward course of duty, and the resolutions of our best moments, to be faithful, steadfast, and immovable.—But it is the part of wisdom and of duty, to give no reasonable ground to suspect evil of our good; and to aim after those things which are of good report. He that is careless of character will not only be forced, as life advances, to *feel* his folly to his cost, but he will in all probability have the temptations to evil increased tenfold. The fear of man sometimes worketh a snare, but the desire of a clear reputation is often a powerful ally to virtue, and an incitement to active and generous efforts, which, in the earlier periods of the spiritual progress, are not generally to be expected without it. Yet does this laudable motive, when inordinate, continually defeat all its best ends. It degenerates into pride and vanity, and corrodes the reputation which was its object. It fetters the mind by the necessity for the good opinion of others as its stimulus; it alloys the best emanations of benevolence; it lowers the tone of moral sentiment; it is the bane of humility, and it calls off from that attention to duty and to the approbation of the Omniscient Judge, which are the best supports of virtue, and the surest motives to the practice of it.—Where reputation is made the ruling object of desire, the higher principles will seldom govern, or their rule will be without firmness, and ever fluctuating with the opinions of the world. A *regard* to reputation may continue, and ought to continue, long after the *desire* of it has ceased to be a leading motive. It is a support of virtue, and often directs to a wise employment of the experience of others. But it is our duty to pursue what is solidly excellent in itself, as well as fair and lovely in the estimation of others; and to live and act as having the eye of God ever upon us, and the example and word of Christ to guide us; influenced by the highest principle, that of obedience to the will of Him who has taught us by His inspired servant, that "the world passeth away, and the lusts thereof, but he that doeth the will of God abideth for ever."

Whatever then is virtuous, whatever deserves approbation, let us make them the object of our earnest solemn purposes, and our steadfast watchful aim; and may the peace of God which passeth all understanding keep our hearts and minds through Jesus Christ.—Amen.

SERMON VIII.

"WE HAVE CORRUPTED NO MAN."

2 CORINTHIANS VII., 2.

RECEIVE US; WE HAVE WRONGED NO MAN, WE HAVE CORRUPTED NO MAN, WE HAVE DEFRAUDED NO MAN.

The Apostle was called upon by the circumstances in which he was placed with respect to the Corinthian Christians, to make these animated and just assertions of the unblameableness of his conduct among them; and it is well for us, if we are able to make the same appeal to our own consciences, and,—in those moments when the world is shut out, and the power of conscience and the convictions of religion are duly felt,—can say with truth, I have wronged no one, I have defrauded no one, *I have corrupted no one.*

Considering how much the social nature of man exposes him to the influence of the immoral words and actions of others, how much they tend to countenance and confirm wrong propensities, to pervert his notions of duty, and to lessen the power of those right views and principles which would conduct him safely to endless happiness, it is required by prudence as well as by religion, that we should be on our guard against the influence of customs and examples, which are inconsistent with the gospel of

Jesus; and it is also required by every principle of benevolence and duty, that we should avoid, as much as lies in our power, whatever may corrupt the Christian principles, and weaken the Christian practice, of others.

It is probable that few pay a sufficient attention to the influence which their conduct and conversation have upon the minds of others; and that persons, whose own character is truly Christian, often do essential injury by unguarded expressions, and by not sufficiently guarding against the appearance of evil. That those who are not desirous to act according to the rules of the Gospel, do frequently and essentially injure the moral character of others, without direct intention, is too obvious to require proof; and it is a fact of the most distressing kind, calculated to give the most painful impressions of the degree to which human depravity may reach, that, in numerous instances, those who do not subject themselves to the restraints of duty intentionally endeavour to lead others into the paths of wickedness; and this too sometimes, without any advantage or pleasure to themselves.

It may be attended with some beneficial effects to our own minds, if we consider, somewhat particularly, cases in which men injure the moral character of others.

The *first* and most striking case is, where men of wicked and abandoned character, with very little temptation of interest or pleasure, intentionally weaken the principles, and place temptation in the way, of those who, without such temptation, might have been preserved from any great and decided departures from duty. Instances have been known where persons, possessed of some pleasing qualities of head or heart, have exercised them with a direct view to lead others from the paths of peace. They have induced them to believe that the way of vice is pleasant,—that there could be no harm in gratifying those propensities which naturally spring up in the human frame. They have applied their efforts to that feeling of false shame, by which thousands and tens of thousands have fallen into the snares of sin. They have endeavoured, with all the arts of persuasive sophistry, to loosen those restraints which religious principles have imposed, to stifle the upbraidings of conscience, and to destroy the dread of futurity. And they have gloried in their fall, and rejoiced to see them become as abandoned as themselves. The young should know that such things are possible, and that such things have too often occurred; but the more common case is,—

Secondly, When persons of abandoned character, principally with a view to their own gratification or interest, (though sometimes, it is to be feared, mixed with wicked satisfaction at their success,) intentionally lead others to partake in their criminal excesses, or induce them to become partners in schemes of dishonesty or malice. Though these cases may not mark such deplorable depravity as those which I last mentioned, there is a degree of wickedness in such conduct, which, should the conscience ever become alive to the sense of duty, will harrow up its inmost recesses, and inflict pangs which they only can fully know, who have experienced the torments of a guilty conscience; and which will, at any rate, in all probability, constitute a chief source of their future misery. Most vices are of a social nature; and he who indulges in them cannot fail sometimes to lead aside the unwary, and to break down the barriers of virtue. And still more frequently must he increase the strength of evil habits in the minds of others, and harden the transgressor in his wickedness. Many persons seem to think that they have a right to sport with their own lives and happiness as they please, provided they do not harm to others; and some of this description have so much of inconsistent benevolence about them, that they would not wilfully inflict pain upon a fellow mortal. And upon this benevolence they pique themselves; while they neglect the Divine commandments, as these respect themselves and their God. Those who are deaf to the voice of religion, when she assures them that a time will come when God will render unto every man according to his works, cannot be expected to listen to those obvious considerations of duty, which force themselves upon the minds of the obedient: or we might tell them, that real benevolence requires that they should not incapacitate themselves from discharging their duty to others; and, above all, that by their criminal excess they were doing more injury to the worth and happiness of those of whose happiness they may think they are tender, than if they were to injure their property, or inflict upon them direct bodily suffering. Does he who first leads the unwary youth into the haunts of debauchery do him no injury?—does he who laughs at his scruples, and aids him to stifle the reproaches of conscience, do him no injury?—does he do him no injury, who countenances him by his example, and, by his licentious language, by his licentious conduct, strengthens those wicked habits, which but for him might have been left so weak that conscience might have regained its once acknowledged dominion? Does he do no harm to his fellow-creature, who makes the first inroads on family purity?—or he who contributes to render the poor wretch an outcast of society?—or he who then encourages her in practices which rivet her in the chains of vice, which make life a burden so long as the slightest sense of duty or honor remains alive, and which, if they extinguish all shame, sink the character to the lowest degree of depravity?

Men wretchedly deceive themselves when they suppose that their vices do no harm to others. They may not be able to see how an *individual* act of wickedness is injurious; but no one has a right to calculate by the effect of individual acts. He who wilfully sins once, is more prepared to fall by temptation, than he was before. The horror attending the first great breach of duty is gone; and to prevent further breaches, those considerations alone remain, which have already proved too weak. And few will be so absurd as to deny that, by frequent acts of wickedness, they must do injury to the minds, if not to the property or present happiness, of others. It appears to me that on this point we are often negligent in our calculations. Moral worth is the only substantial ground of peace here, and is essentially requisite to happiness in that uncertain state whither we are all hastening. He, then, who does what will deprave another or increase his depravity, does him the most essential injury. He may be himself called from the paths of sin; he may then use his utmost efforts to undo the wrong which he has done; but this cannot be. The sins of that other will have in like manner depraved others, or increased *their* depravity; and so prolific is the nature of vice, that one crime has often given birth to a thousand others: and no one can truly say, that the consequences of his ill conduct shall go no further.

If there should be any now present, who make it no object to submit their conduct to the restraints prescribed by the laws of our Heavenly Father, let me entreat them to consider, that the commands of a wise and benevolent God cannot be violated without evil consequences; for they must be designed to prevent evils, and He who has ordained them will vindicate their importance. If in this life they are not forced to perceive that no breach of duty is harmless, that those indulgencies in conduct, forbidden by the laws of God, which they flattered themselves injured no one, have never been without consequences baneful to their own peace and worth, baneful to the peace and worth of others,—the time will come when the ruinous consequences of sin will teach them its real enormity, when they will learn to perceive how unjustly and how foolishly, and how presumptuously they reasoned, when they dared to suppose that to do what God has forbidden would do harm to no one. Indeed there is but one complete safeguard from the deceitful sophistry of vicious inclinations; it is to repress their false representations by the considerations of religion. Reflect whether God can approve of the conduct to which they prompt; and if not, be assured that it is sinful, and that, however pleasing its appearance, it cannot fail to be injurious to your best interests, and in all probability to the best interests of others. Were the young but heartily and habitually impressed with the conviction, that God knows all our thoughts and actions, and that obedience to His will is in all cases our duty, and in all cases our true wisdom, they would have a support to virtuous principles and dispositions, which would usually enable those to stand firm in the day of trial, and give them a general decision, vigour, and permanency.

But let us consider a little the manner in which the moral worth of others may be injured by a *third* class, of those who essentially corrupt the moral principles of others by their opinions and practices. It consists of those inconsiderate persons who, without thinking of the evil which they do, or paying any direct attention to the rules of duty, go on in the round of dissipation, heedless of their final destination, and regardless of the purposes for which they were sent into the world. Those persons pass their days without any serious thought. They would not perhaps willingly do anything which they thought to be harm; and, so long as they keep clear of those things, believe that they are at least as good as their neighbours. But God is not in all their thoughts; duty and a life to come are forgotten in the round of amusement and apparent gaiety. They may possess many engaging qualities of head and heart; many of which, if they had been planted in a more kindly soil, would have taken a deep root and brought forth fruit to everlasting life. And by those engaging qualities, and by the general influence of their language and example, numbers are led into the same fatal delusion, and live as though this life were their all, spending one day after another as though they were to live for ever, without making any preparation for that world, where nothing will avail but the possession of right affections of heart, and the faithful endeavour to discharge duty as far as known to us. Persons of this class not only injure others by their neglect of Christian duty, but also, and this in a most essential degree, by ridiculing strict attention and even any tolerable attention to religion, by insinuating, if not expressly conveying, that they regard religious duty as unfashionable, and stigmatizing those who avoid the usual amusements, and frivolous levity, with which the Lord's day is spent, as sanctified censors of those who merely do as others do.

In general it is to be feared, that persons who devote the best of their time and affections to the trifling pursuit of trifling pleasures, at that period when the affections usually receive their lasting bias, and when, if at any time, the foundation is laid for genuine worth, will leave life without any suitable preparation for eternity. Happy would it be for them, if their last days, if their futurity, were not embittered by the recollections, that they have not only wasted their own lives, but led others to waste theirs.

Fourthly,—And (among those who are likely to be influenced by the Christian preacher,) a more prevalent class,—those who have the sense of duty sufficiently strong to preserve them from flagrant sins, but who yet do not make a point of considering and obeying its dictates in all cases; who have a general sense of religion and of the importance of it, and have no acknowledged wish to throw off its restraints, but who yet do not make it an object of primary concern, (allowing other inferior objects to have a greater share in their heart's attention,) and do not sincerely try to obey God in all things. Whether we, my friends, are in this class, is a point which it will be well for us to determine; for if we are, our situation and character are very dubious. But to aid you in this inquiry, is not my present object; it is rather to point out how persons of this class (and even, in some of the cases, persons who really are sincerely endeavouring to serve and please God,) may corrupt others by their words or actions.

In the first place, the degree of indifference to religious duties which is so often manifested by professing Christians, necessarily produces in the minds of others the idea, that religion is not so necessary or so pleasant as the Scriptures represent it to be. They see such persons maintain a general respectability of character, they perceive that they keep aloof from all gross and observed immorality, and perhaps have reason to believe that their general conduct in society is consistent with the rules of the gospel; but at the same time they perceive that the public or private discharge of the duties of religion, by which, and by which only, religious principle is generally kept alive in the heart, is made of little consideration,—often neglected,—and, when attended to, attended to with apparent indifference or levity. These things (which, however, sometimes may be in appearance only,) have very frequently given rise to the idea, that religion is not essential; that it is not necessary to be so very good; and that, so long as there is nothing wrong in the conduct, no direct breach of the duties which we owe to our fellow-creatures, all is right, and the hope of final acceptance may be rightly indulged. It should be ever borne in mind, by those who feel such opinions influence their conduct, that it is to actions, only as springing from right dispositions of heart, that the gospel promises its reward;—that in all probability there never was an instance where the duties of morality (as they respect ourselves or other men) where in any great degree strictly, faithfully, and fully discharged, where there was not a considerable degree of religious principle;—that at any rate, (even supposing the virtues of benevolence and self-government to have gained a high degree of strength and vigour in the heart,) yet the gospel requires not only love to men, but love to God, not only morality in the common sense of the term, but the spirit of disposition of Christ, in which most assuredly obedience to the will of God as such constituted the ruling feature;—and lastly, that the happiness of the blessed must necessarily consist in the exercise of the best affections of our nature, and in a peculiar manner of those which have God for their object; and consequently, that those persons cannot be fit to be partakers of that happiness, who have lived in the habitual and allowed neglect of the devout affections.

But, secondly, from that fear and love of the world, which are almost alike at enmity with the love and fear of God, persons who really have considerable sense of religion, and in many respects endeavour to obey its dictates, often injure the moral worth of others, by want of steady opposition to what they know to be wrong; by countenancing by their words or actions, customs and practices which they disapprove, but which they have not strength of mind to resist; by listening without any appearance of disapprobation (and even sometimes with an apparent assent to the ridicule thrown upon those who manifest a strict regard to Christian principle,) to the language of impurity, and to principles which tend to sap the foundation of purity and religion in the minds of others.

Again, thirdly, persons who are not themselves strict in their regard to religious principle, frequently injure others by themselves advancing opinions, which, though they may be harmless in their own minds, yet are essentially injurious to those in whose minds moral principle has not taken a firm root. Such opinions may be true, and may naturally follow from others indisputably true; and, when taken in their just extent, and also limited by the restrictions which the moralist would impose upon them, may be practically beneficial, but when taken unconnectedly must be hurtful, and lead the young and unexperienced to conclusions very injurious to their peace and virtue. Those who do really believe that Jesus Christ was sent by God, and spoke with the authority of God, ought to regard with suspicion every moral principle, which is, even in appearance, opposed by the spirit of precepts of his Gospel; and at any rate, it should be their endeavour so to guard their own words, that they may not be supposed to justify or teach practices, which they must consider as expressly discountenanced by him who was the Word of God.

A fourth way in which persons, who are not seriously disposed to make obedience to God and duty their primary object, corrupt others, is, by indulging themselves freely in those gratifications and amusements, from which perhaps they may derive no injury, but by which in all probability others would be injured.—Whatever practices and amusements, are usually attended with injurious consequences to the moral character of others, whether or not they are necessarily so,—to countenance them is in reality to expose ourselves to the guilt of those consequences: and if those practices or amusements not only usually are attended with such injurious consequences, but are never unattended with great and serious evils,—however innocent they may be to ourselves alone, we are not justifiable in setting others the example of engaging in them, and thus saying, if not in words, still more forcibly by our conduct, there is no harm in them. It is not to be expected that others will reason so nicely respecting our actions, and from our actions to our opinions, as we ourselves do. He who sees the professing Christian freely indulge in any practice or amusement which suits his inclination, will very gladly take his example as his precedent. "There can be no harm in this," he will naturally, but probably absurdly, say in reply to the suggestions of a more rigid adviser, "for those who have as much religion as yourself, without any hesitation do as I do." Can it be expected that those nice distinctions will be attended to, on which the morality of the practice or amusement depends?—or will it not almost necessarily happen, that the general features of the circumstances only will be attended to, and the fact, that we pursue such and such a plan of conduct, be alone regarded?

These considerations might be pursued to a much greater length; but they are all modifications of the general principle, that the professing Christian must necessarily injure the moral worth of others, whenever and however he advances opinions which are inconsistent with the strict morality of the Gospel, and whenever he manifests a practical disregard to the spirit and precepts of Jesus. And it cannot be too strongly impressed upon our minds, that we shall be called to give an account, not only of our actions but of our words; and that, where the consequences of our words and actions are naturally injurious to others, (whether or not those consequences actually follow; though in general we are incompetent judges of this,) we are answerable for those consequences; and that therefore it is our bounden duty, for the sake of others as well as ourselves, to endeavour to make our conduct and conversation so consistent with the spirit and precept of the Gospel, that, when we stand before His bar, it may not add to our personal offences against His law, that we have, by our opinions or by our practices, weakened the religious strength of any, assisted to stifle the reproaches of conscience, or afforded to the wicked encouragement in their wickedness.

I wish the younger part of my hearers in particular, to direct their attention to three observations which naturally arise from this subject; with which I will conclude.

1. It is of the first importance to their future peace of mind, and to save them from some of the severest pangs which can arise in the awakened conscience, that they should carefully avoid whatever, either in their words or actions, will tend to corrupt those around them or increase their corruption. The first impulse to youthful vices, has often been the vicious language or conduct of thoughtless companions, who perhaps may have directly intended no harm, but who have in reality done the greatest injury.

2. It is your duty as well as wisdom, to shun, as dangerous enemies to your best interests, those companions who, in their conversation and conduct, manifest a want of that restraint which the Gospel of Jesus imposes upon criminal propensities,—a restraint which never yet, where fully submitted to, injured the happiness of any,—and which never yet was thrown off without the most baneful effects upon the peace and real welfare of the present life, and upon the happiness of that to come.

3. Let me implore of you to bear in mind, that the evil practices and opinions of others, will furnish no excuse for you at that awful day, when God will judge the

world in righteousness, and will render unto every man according to his works. That day will in effect be present to each of us, when life leaves us; and then every one must bear his own burden. You have a clear rule of duty,—the words of Jesus, and of those who were sent by him to teach his religion. The words of Jesus are the words of God; they claim your attentive regard and obedience. If you make the rules of duty, as they are contained in the Scriptures, your guide, they will conduct you safely through the journey of life; they will prevent no innocent pleasure; they will increase every joy which has a title to the heart; they will support you under its difficulties and trials; they will cheer you in the near prospect of dissolution; and through the ages of eternity, (gracious God, what infinite rewards hast Thou promised to our poor services!) through the countless ages of eternity, you will enjoy happiness beyond the utmost grasp of human imagination.

But let me remind you, too, of the alternative. If you neglect the various warnings which are afforded you, of your duty and destination,—if you begin, with the presumptuous hope that you will but begin, and continue, as there is then too much reason to fear that you will, in the way which the wicked, and which you too, may call pleasure, but which in reality leadeth to destruction;—I have nothing to present to you but the terrors of the Lord; for indignation and wrath, tribulation and anguish, will be upon the soul of every one who doeth evil. May God of His great mercy preserve us all from this dreadful state.

SERMON IX.

CHRISTIAN PATRIOTISM.*

Christian Brethren,

The occurrences of the past week have recalled, in the hearts of millions, all that vividness of loyal sentiment with which we first welcomed our young Sovereign to the station appointed her by the providence of Him who is Lord of all;—a sentiment raised into affection, and strengthened into attachment, by various traits in her public conduct during the first year of regal duty, and by the increased knowledge which we have had of her personal character, of the principles by which her education was regulated, and of the fixedness of those purposes which, on the day of her accession, she declared with an earnestness that filled our hearts with joy.

The recent solemn acts, by which the nation distinctly recognizes her as its Sovereign, and pledges its fealty to her, and by which she expressly undertakes the high duties of her trust, under a sense of her responsibilities, and under the impressive and inviolable engagements of

---

* This discourse was preached in Lewin's Mead Chapel, on the Sunday after the Coronation of Her Majesty Queen Victoria, June 28th, 1838. It was dedicated to her mother, the Duchess of Kent.

religion, may well direct us to consider our own duties as members of the civil community of which she is the appointed head and bond of union; and I hope for your serious attention, while I lead you to a train of thought which is in no way unsuitable for occasional introduction when we thus meet together to worship our common Father, but which may be deemed peculiarly appropriate to our present circumstances, and may be profitable to us as Christians,—for the duty of the Christian extends to every relation in life.

With such views I desire to offer you my sentiments on the nature and requirements of Christian patriotism; and I know not how I can now better introduce them, than by a reference to the closing expression in those words which the aged Simeon uttered,[*] when the child Jesus was presented in the temple. " Then took he him up in his arms, and blessed God, and said, Lord! now lettest thou thy servant depart in peace, according to thy word; for mine eyes have seen thy salvation, which thou hast prepared before the face of all people;—a light to ligthen the Gentiles, and the glory of thy people Israel."

THE GLORY OF THY PEOPLE ISRAEL. (Luke ii. 32.)

In the prosecution of my design I shall, in the first place, offer some considerations respecting the duty of patriotism, in connection with the teachings of the Scriptures; secondly, give, in some detail, my views respecting the nature and influences of Christian patriotism; and, in the third place, state some of those manifestations of it, which, in my judgment, may be expected from one

[*] Luke ii. 28—32.

so trained, and so disposed, as is the young Sovereign of these realms.*

I. Our present purpose does not lead us specifically to contemplate the inestimable blessings which the Saviour of all men came to confer upon every child of mortality, but to view his relation to his own people; not to dwell upon his love to all the world, but to survey that affection which he manifested to the country of his birth. Listen to his words, recorded by the same Evangelist, when, on approaching Jerusalem to finish the work assigned to him by his Heavenly Father, in the midst of the joyous acclamations of the multitudes, hailing him as the promised King of Israel, he wept at the sight of the city, and said, "If thou hadst known, at least in this thy day, the things which belong unto thy peace! but now they are hid from thine eyes."†

Who that contemplates this scene, can doubt that the *love of country* formed one of those enlarged and elevated affections which filled the breast of him who loved all mankind? And who that seeks for his duty, not merely in the express precepts, but also in the spirit of Christ, can hesitate in regarding *patriotism* as a virtue? Yet have there been some who have censured the Christian religion, because (they say) it does not inculcate this affection. Others again have spurned the affection itself; and have contended that it ought not to have place in the character of the *Christian*. And more still have looked upon it with a suspicious eye; and in their zeal for the welfare of *man-*

---

* This third part of the sermon is here omitted, as inappropriate at the present distance of time.

† Luke xix. 42.

kind, have practically forgotten that the good of *all* can only be promoted by each promoting the good of some. * * *

In that character in which contrasted virtues, seldom found combined, were all united and blended in delightful harmony,—all shown to be consistent, when in their just proportion and relation,—we find the strong features of genuine patriotism in no degree obliterated, but, on the contrary, made more glowing and resplendent by that universal benevolence taught him by his love to God, as well as by the great purposes for which he came. He who was to be the Saviour of all men, could not but love all men. He was the light of the world, the effulgence of that universal Parent whose sun of divine bounty riseth on the evil and on the good; and it was not possible that the beams of his affection, any more than those of the love and mercy which he came to offer to all the sons of men, should be confined to the little spot where "the sun of righteousness" actually arose. But it is among the proofs of the merciful adaptation of the Gospel to such a being as man,—who is first to imbibe love at the bosom which nourishes and cherishes him, and to proceed from the domestic charities to the love of neighbour, and from the love of friends to advance to the love of enemies, and from the love of country to expand his heart to the love of all mankind,—that he who showed us benevolence in its purest, most disinterested, most ennobling, most comprehensive forms, manifested also its elementary affections; that he, in whose heart love was like the ocean, has enabled us to trace the copious springs from which much of its waters proceed. Because he loved God, and God loveth all, he loved all, and died for all: yet the closer bonds of human nature were also felt by him, and proved to be consistent with the sublimest benevolence. He felt the endearing regards of friendship; for "he loved Martha and her sister, and Lazarus." He felt the ties of filial affection—ties which cannot be dissolved without evil and degradation somewhere; for in his expiring agonies, with tenderness deep but calm, he commended his mother to the care of the beloved disciple. He felt compassion for the sorrows which he was going to relieve, and wept with those whose tears he was about to dry up. And the calamities which he had laboured to avert from his country, excluded all thoughts of himself. When the women who followed him on the way to calvary were bewailing him, "Daughters of Jerusalem, weep not for me, but weep for yourselves and your children," was the affecting expression of true patriotism; and that noble supplication which shows the victory over every feeling of self, "Father! forgive them, for they know not what they do," breathes also the prayer, that still his country might be saved from the overwhelming ruin which his enemies had just imprecated upon themselves and upon their children, and which he had laboured to avert. "O Jerusalem, Jerusalem, which killest the prophets, and stonest them which are sent unto thee! how often would I have gathered thy children together, as a hen doth gather her brood under her wings, and ye would not!"

II. Such is real patriotism. He who loves his country with the love of principle and knowledge, will not love it the less because he endeavours to make Christ his guide in all things.

There is, indeed, a love of one's country which is little more than an instinctive principle, without object, restraint, enlightenment, or expansion. Even this is not without its use, if it carry the mind out of itself; and, in most persons, it is perhaps the earliest stage of that generous and exalted principle which alone deserves the appellation of patriotism. On the other hand, it often perverts the sense of justice; it makes men forget that other nations have rights as well as their own; and that the all-comprehensive principle of Christian equity should be made the guide in the transactions and intercourse of nations, as well as in those of individuals. But so also is there a parental feeling which is more like an instinct of nature than an affection of reason; prompting strongly, but without any view to the distant good of the object of it; thwarting the desire of enlightened benevolence; and leading to consult the little caprices and fancied rights of childhood, at the expense of justice and of wisdom,— All the natural affections require the guidance and purifying influence of religion; and the comprehensive views of the Gospel, taking in all the world, and taking in both worlds, do give to the more limited charities that direction, and expansion, and refinement, which, without them, these could scarcely know.

Christian patriotism will be just to other nations. Even among that people of ancient times, whose misguided love of their country led to exalt her empire on the ruin of all others, and whose ambition—though, in the unsearchable plans of Providence, the means of preparing for the kingdom of peace and love—continually violated the plainest principles of humanity, and trampled upon the rights of all around her, the enlightened ruler and philosopher taught, and many of less commanding power acted upon the principle, that justice was to be observed towards their enemies,—all being accounted enemies by the Romans, who were not subjects or submissive allies. The world has sometimes called those patriots, who have promoted, or attempted to promote, their country's aggrandisement, by violation of treaties, by falsehood, and by treachery, by the careless and causeless invasion of the peace and welfare of neighbouring nations, and by various other means, which, in the narrower walks of life, would make a man detested and shunned: but this is not Christian patriotism. Christian patriotism must be founded on the everlasting maxim of equity, "Whatsoever ye would that men should do unto you, do ye even so unto them." He who possesses this elevated disposition, will seek to promote the interests of his own nation; but he will never do it by unchristian means.

It is a grand idea—and the increasing acknowledgment of it, however inconsistently maintained among those who had influence over the public mind, or in our national councils, was one of the proofs of a rapidly increasing diffusion of enlightened principle, which while contemplating the fearful prospects of national calamity which the older among us have witnessed, cheered the heart with the hope that all would yet be well with our suffering and offending country; it is a grand idea, that nations are members of one great community, with common interests and with common rights; that no plea of ambition, or of selfish advantage, can justly be permitted to encroach upon those rights and interests; and that no great and continued encroachment can be made upon them, without meeting with its appropriate punishment. The principle is as just as it is grand. Such subjects seldom come under our consideration from the pulpit; and I will take the opportunity to read a passage from a public document, in which these sound and comprehensive views are recognized, and which proves that they are not the theories of the speculative enthusiast, but the maxims of enlightened experience. It occurs in the address which Washington, when he closed his career of solid glory, by voluntarily retiring from power, published as a last legacy to his country, and which is a record of political wisdom, not surpassed, and probably unequalled, in ancient or in modern times.

"Observe good faith and justice," says the father of the people, "towards all nations: cultivate peace and harmony with all. Religion and morality enjoin this conduct; and can it be that good policy does not equally enjoin it? It will be worthy of a free, enlightened, and great nation, to give to mankind the magnanimous and too novel example, of a people always guided by an exalted justice and benevolence. Who can doubt, that in the course of time and things, the fruit of such a plan would richly repay any temporary advantage which might be lost by a steady adherence to it? Can it be that Providence has not connected the permanent felicity of a nation with its virtues?"

You must agree with me, my hearers, in thinking that such principles should be inscribed on the heart of every one who loves his country, and has any means of promoting its welfare.

Christian patriotism, while it desires to promote, and must first promote, the welfare of its own community, will cherish a feeling sense of compassion to the wants and distresses of other nations. Modified, as patriotism ever will be in the breast where Gospel principles reside, by that philanthropy which sees a neighbour in every one to whom it can stretch out the arm to protect or the hand to cure, the Christian's love for his country, glowing *there* with most vivid flames, where it can best direct its vital warmth and influence, will extend to *all* the desire to do good as there is opportunity, and will, according to the talents possessed, employ those means of carrying it into effective operation, which the powerful engines of the present times afford in aid of individual exertion. National ambition must exist while men bear the image of the earthy; but in proportion as they put on the image of the heavenly, will it aim to raise its country among surrounding nations, by the influence of its justice, its good faith, its humanity; by seeking, not its own prosperity alone, but the welfare of others also; by the victories, not of its arms, but of its arts, its knowledge, its wisdom, and its virtues. In this noble career, the love of country will advance with the love of mankind; for what exalts our own, must contribute to raise others also. Human well-being is not a stock which is lessened by those who enjoy it as they ought. In a family, that member has the most happiness who shares it most in common with every other; and every one wisely promoting his own, will be promoting at the same time the happiness of all. In a state, the man who grows rich by the upright employment of enterprise, ability, and industry, contributes to the general wealth far beyond his own personal gains. And every nation rising thus in the scale of knowledge, wisdom, and virtue, will assist by its influence, and by its example, to raise others also.

Perhaps there is no nation that has ever taken so high a rank in this respect as our own: and while religious philanthropy rejoices at contemplating the mighty machines by which millions are enabled to aid in spreading the knowledge of salvation, and an acquaintance with those Scriptures which contain the knowledge and the terms; by which the links of union between man and man are extended beyond all previous anticipation, and those whom the eye will never see, nor the ear hear, in this world, are aided in their journey heavenward;—and while religious philosophy, observing the astonishing efforts of benevolence which unexampled evils have caused, and the amazing development of energy and extension of knowledge to which the storms of the political world have so powerfully contributed, rejoices to trace the way in which He who directs the storm is bringing good out of evil;—Christian patriotism can also rejoice, that amidst much that our nation has done which she should wish undone, and much that she has left undone which she should have done, and large as her share in the work of destruction, and eager as her aspirings after earthly aggrandisement, she has taken a high and dignified station in those great objects which secure the rights and welfare of man, and which embrace the interests of the whole human race.

II. But while Christian patriotism is thus extended, and elevated, and refined, by the precepts and example of him who taught us who our neighbour is, and instructed us to pray that the kingdom of God may come, and His will be done on earth as it is in heaven, it is in no degree directed by them to forget its own immediate duties: and in all these it fully coincides with the directions of the Gospel, simply applying these to the relation in which we stand to others as members of civil society, and to the community of which we are members.

Its first duty is ALLEGIANCE, or an enlightened respect to the law, and obedience to the constituted authorities. This certainly does not require that we should be blind to the defects of our laws, or without solicitude for their improvement; or that we should not watch over the execution of them, and the direction of legal power. On the contrary, an enlightened love of our country will prompt us, as we have opportunity, to extend the knowledge and observance of those principles on which all our laws and all our political institutions should be founded, by which they should be guided, and to which they should be reduced. All these may be summed up in one word, the common welfare. All laws should have this object, and all power should be regarded as a trust to accomplish it. A warm and enlightened attachment to our political institutions, is perfectly consistent with an earnest desire to see their abuses corrected, and with the employment of those means which the general diffusion of knowledge has rendered so powerful to effect their extension and their utility. It is, for instance, the duty of every one who believes that the rights of any class of the community are unnecessarily shackled, or that the ends of justice are not answered by the penal statutes of his country, to contribute what he can to the enlightenment of public opinion, and by the persevering employment of calm and temperate effort, to improve and correct, and thereby to avert evil. But the common welfare too immediately and obviously depends upon the maintenance of the principle of allegiance, to allow him to be regarded as otherwise than a violator of the rights of society, and a destroyer of the blessings of civil order and peace, who does not himself maintain it, or who leads others to violate it.

Allegiance is a principle of comprehensive operation. It begins in the narrow relations of life, and thence expands, promoting, as it advances, the good order and peace of every little community in which it exists. It is cherished in a family, where children learn to " obey their parents in the Lord." It is cherished in every seminary for training the youthful mind, where order, and cheerful submission, and regard to the rights of those around, are taught and observed. It is cherished, wherever, in the relation of servant and master, or of inferior depending upon a superior, are maintained the duties of wise subordination and good fidelity; and it is cherished, too, wherever, in those various relations, the superior manifests a kind and thoughtful consideration of the welfare of those on whose services he has a claim; respects their conscientious exercise of those rights over which he has no just control; and aims, in the spirit of love, to make obedience a principle of the heart, and not the submission of the slave.

Closely connected with the principle of allegiance is that of LOYALTY, including the sentiment of attachment to the person in whom, as supreme, is vested the government of the country by the execution of its laws, and by faithfulness to the duties which arise from the relation existing between him and the people. It prompts to the obedience of duty; but it has nothing in common with that blind subjection which is yielded, through necessity, to the tyrant. It sometimes leads to the noblest self-devotement; but it does not resemble that prostration of spirit to the irresistible decrees of the despot, which impels to give up life at his mandate, without a struggle, and to welcome the message of death as conferring honour and happiness. It has within it the germ of ennobling enthusiasm; but it is an enthusiasm which does not spring from the dazzled imagination and the heated feelings, but which rests on the sound exercise of the judgment, and receives its fullest approval. It views the sovereign as the sovereign of right, and not of might; as virtually deriving his power from those for whose welfare he is to employ it; as holding a station most important and honourable, but involving most serious responsibilities; as having a claim upon the obedience and co-operation of his subjects, for their own individual benefit, and for the good of the community at large, as well as for his own happiness; as having a claim, too, upon their candour in judging of his motives and his conduct; as, in return, under the obligation of duty to listen to their petitions, and even to their remonstrances, and, as far as the most comprehensive views of public welfare will permit, to be influenced by them; as virtually accountable to them for the right use of his high powers; but, above all, as accountable to that Being whose providence hath invested him with them. The heart in which such loyalty resides, will rejoice in the personal welfare, and sympathize in the personal sorrows, of the Sovereign; and just in proportion to the personal excellencies that mark his character, and to the indications of devotedness to duty afforded by his public conduct, will be that moral attachment which glows with the more earnestness through the perception of the amount of good which he may achieve, and which, existing in the highly-principled and reflective mind as an element of its own consciousness, becomes more fixed and intense from the knowledge that myriads participate in it.

Christian patriotism will never look with jealousy and envy on the advantages of another nation, yet must it view with peculiar complacency whatever promotes the welfare of its own : it can best understand what elements are essential to its prosperity : it can do most to promote it. The views of the Gospel will often lead to a different estimate of prosperity from what the world might form without it; but Christian patriotism may well rejoice in every thing that indicates improvement in social life, in national industry, in public zeal, in the expansion of public talent, in the promotion of the arts and sciences, in the products of national skill, and in that spirit of enterprise, and ardour of benevolent exertion, by which the advantages of its own country will be increasingly extended beyond the limits of its political sway.

With peculiar delight must Christian patriotism dwell on the promotion of those momentous objects of benevolence and religion, which, in proportion as they are effected, must contribute to the righteousness, on which alone, as a permanent and secure foundation, the great edifice of national welfare can be erected. So complicated are now the relations of social life, so extensive its mutual connections, that whatever achieves improvement in one direction, will eventually have its efficacy in others ; and as no one can labour in every field, it is well that each should devote what talent he possesses to that in which a wise discretion tells him he can labour with effect. Should he feel that he is doing but little, when he compares the rill which he aims to conduct from the fountain of

Christian love, with the majestic stream of public benevolence, yet let him remember that *this* comes from individual hearts.—That the great machine of social well-being may go on in its most perfect state, it is requisite that every spring should act, and every wheel should move, in its due time and relation. If we cannot discern how our respective parts are connected with the interests of the whole, we cannot but perceive that they are with those of the little combination around us; and we may go on in our respective spheres of action with the full security, that while we are, in them, promoting peace, good order, and improvement, we are effectually contributing to the peace, the good order, and the improvement of that great sphere which comprehends all. Nor should we ever permit ourselves to repine that we are not placed in more dignified stations of usefulness, and gifted with more commanding powers; still less to envy and depreciate the success of those who are entrusted with higher talents. "Charity envieth not;" and Christian patriotism, which rises above the distinction of sect and party, and exists in every one, will rejoice at all which is accomplished by others to promote its great purposes; and where it cannot itself labour, it will aid, by sympathy, and by dispersing from the breasts of others the chilling influences of indifference, to cheer the hearts, and to strengthen the hands, of those who can.

Nevertheless, the numerous combinations of individuals to accomplish good for which solitary benevolence would be ineffectual, present to us means for personal exertion, or for pecuniary aid, which only require selection, and which leave no excuse for him who wraps up his talent in a napkin. The great purposes of benevolence are, to remove or lessen evil, and to prevent its entrance or its spread; and if you can effectually lessen the distresses of want and sickness; if you can aid the paralyzed arm of industry; if you can reclaim the wanderer from the fold of Christ, or restore to his country the offender against its laws; if you can assist in preparing the young for the duties of society, and in training them for the highest purposes of a life that is to leave its impress on eternity,—or, where all these are really out of your power, if, in the domestic relations, and in the wider connections of our social nature, you teach by precept and example the duties of the Gospel, the best guide to human welfare,—you are benefactors of your country. Pitiable must be the feelings of him who can look back upon no thoughtful persevering effort to do good in his day and generation, and who is obliged to acknowledge, that if the world is better, it is not through him, even if he have done nothing to make it worse.

III. There is one in these lands, respecting whose power for good, or for evil,—great beyond ordinary appreciation,—no one can doubt; and who must often contemplate the possession of it with a religious solicitude that cannot but give earnestness to the prayer for the guidance and blessing of Almighty God,—earnestness to the supplication,—" Deliver us from evil." * * *

You will, I doubt not, as a Christian congregation, unite with me in commending Her Majesty to the protection, guidance, and blessing of the God and Father of all, in the name of our Lord and Saviour Jesus Christ. May she be preserved from the moral dangers which must ever attend the elevated rank and power assigned to the earthly Sovereign by the Lord of all worlds and beings.

May she be enabled to carry into effect her purposes of wisdom and benevolence, in the improvement of our national institutions, and the extension of national prosperity. If it please the Supreme Disposer, may her reign be continued, with true happiness and glory to herself, through a long succession of years; and when most of us shall be gathered to our fathers, may the general welfare be effectually promoted by her just and beneficent sway. When the termination of this arrives, and that cometh to her which is appointed to all, may she be found fully prepared to give a good account to that Master to whom it is the highest honour of the most elevated of mankind to be faithful servants; and, for an earthly crown, receive one that fadeth not away.

SERMON X.

THE YOUNG EXHORTED TO WALK IN THE GOOD OLD WAY.

JEREMIAH VI., 16.

THUS SAITH THE LORD, STAND YE IN THE WAYS, AND SEE, AND ASK FOR THE OLD PATHS, WHERE IS THE GOOD WAY, AND WALK THEREIN, AND YE SHALL FIND REST FOR YOUR SOULS.

ONE of the most instructive fables of heathen antiquity, represents Hercules (when arrived at years of reflection) as retiring into a solitary place to consider his future course of life. There, we are told, he was accosted by two females, one named Virtue, and the other Pleasure; each of whom was desirous to prevail upon him to join her votaries. Pleasure presented to him her various allurements, and offered to him a life of ease and indulgence. Virtue displayed to him the fallacy of her rival's pretensions, and showed him that true happiness could be found only in *her* service.—She did not however attempt to deceive him by false expectations: she fairly told him that he would have to overcome difficulties; to pass through various trials; to exercise fortitude and self-denial; to make many sacrifices; and to undergo many labours and dangers: but then it would not be for nothing. She showed him that, by the wise appointment of the gods, there was no valuable object of pursuit which was to be acquired by any other means; and that thus alone he could gain the applause and esteem of the wise and good, the pleasures of self-approbation, and the favour of the gods. Hercules, we are told, was decided by her representations; and his decision was a wise one.

Those who have had common advantages for the acquisition of religious knowledge, cannot possibly doubt to which course wisdom directs, (whether that of religious duty, or the broad way in which so many walk, eagerly pursuing the present gratifications of interest or of pleasure); yet it is only as experience enlightens and extends the views of the individual, that he sees the *wisdom* of virtue, and the *folly and danger* of vice, in their just nature and degree. It is utterly impossible to engraft upon the minds of the young, (however well disposed,) all those impressive views which prove to the experienced observer, that godliness hath the promise of the life that now is, as well as of that which is to come. With the infatuation of folly, they sometimes regard his representations as merely designed to throw a gloom over the period of cheerfulness; and (by a natural but most unhappy exaggeration) they mistake the sober lessons of prudence and religion, for the severe austerity of the monk, or the superstition of the devotee. Where the mind has not been early trained to that self-control, which (by one whose want of it ruined his fair prospects of reputation and happiness, and brought him to an untimely grave,) was pronounced to be wisdom's root,—where the young have not, by early discipline, instruction, and example, been taught to look beyond the mere present ends of their conduct, to seek for some higher object than mere gratification, to consult some other rule than the mere caprice or impulse of the moment, —where, in short, they have not had impressed upon their hearts that fear of God which is the beginning of Wisdom, —there is little room to hope, but that they will make the experiment for themselves, and find by their own wretched experience, by the loss of health, of reputation, of internal satisfaction, that it is an invariable law of the moral government of God, that peace is not to be found in the paths of wickedness. For such we can only hope and pray, that they may early receive some check in the career of vice: and that the seeds which, in early life, may have been received into the mind, without producing much fruit, which may even seem to have been lost or destroyed, may revive and take a deep root, under the influence of affliction or some other warning of Providence; and in their turn acquire the leading power in the mind. Were it not for the hope that such might eventually be the case, often must the religious parent or friend look forward with the most melancholy apprehension, and see nothing to comfort under the painful emotions of the present.

But there are many who reach the years of reflection, led along, by the gentle hand of parental tenderness, in the good old way. Little exposed to difficulty and trial they are good and virtuous, because out of the way of evil. Their principles have been but little called into exercise; and it is not easy to know their strength. There is room for hope; but there is also much room for solicitude. Their dispositions are good, their tempers amiable, and their present habits favourable to duty. But nothing has yet given them that decision of principle, which can only be acquired by trial. It sometimes happens that their very loveliness of character exposes them to peculiar temptations; and, at any rate, it is impossible for them to make much progress in life, without having in various ways to encounter those snares and dangers, by which many, of as fair promise as themselves, have made shipwreck of a good conscience.

There is still another and a higher class:—those who not only have been led in the ways of wisdom, but have been early taught that most difficult of all lessons, to subdue themselves:—who, without having had their spirits broken, or their vivacity destroyed, have had early impressed on their hearts a sense of religious duty:—who have been taught by every means, which parental affection and experience could suggest, to fear the Lord betimes, to think of obedience to His will as their first and chief concern, and in some good measure to make the directions of religion the habitual guide of their conduct. The foundation has been well laid for truth, for integrity, for purity, for sobriety, for benevolence, for piety: and though he who knows the difficulties and dangers of the journey of life, will not even in such cases be too confident in his expectations, he will feel that there is good room for hope. He may indulge the hope that, by the habitual use of those means by which alone religion can have its proper influence in the heart, it will maintain the ground which it has obtained, will be a lamp unto the feet and a light unto the path, will keep the feet from stumbling, and will direct them in the paths of everlasting peace.

Between these different classes, there are numerous gradations: and I hope there are many among my young hearers, who have upon their minds a prevailing desire to live a virtuous and Christian life. I hope there are many who have not their course wholly to choose; but who have determined that, with the blessing of God, they will walk in the path which their Saviour has pointed out to them, and in which he trod before them.—There may also be others who have not yet thought much on the subject; but whose purposes, as far as they can be said to have been formed, are also favourable to the dictates of duty. —I have nothing now to say to the dissipated and the dissolute, to those who yield up their hearts without restraint to the follies and vices of their profligate and abandoned companions, or who have little or no sense of religion to check their wild career. To such (if any of those now present are unhappily of this class) what I have now to say can be attended with little effect. My object is not to show you the wisdom, the necessity, of living in the fear of God; but to assist you a little in doing so.—And to all among you, to whom experience has not yet rendered advice and exhortation unnecessary, and whose dispositions and intentions are on the side of religion, I wish to offer a few suggestions of religious prudence, which may aid in preserving them from those evils, which to others have proved so injurious, and in some cases so fatal, which have "wounded their consciences and weakened their religious strength," and sometimes made them fall to rise no more.—To such I would say, in the sentiments of the prophet, "Stand ye in the way and see," carefully consider the path in which you are going, whether it is in reality the right one: ask for the good old way,—the way which religious wisdom hath long ago prescribed, and which God hath always owned and blessed. And then "walk therein," resolve to keep close to that way, proceed, and persevere therein: and (as the pious Henry well observes on the text) "you will find that your walking in that way will be easy and pleasant; you will enjoy both your God and yourselves; and the way will lead you to true rest. Though it cost you some pains to walk in that way, you will find an abundant recompense at your journey's end.

In accordance with the direction in my text, let me exhort you;—

1. To consider it as an object of great importance, to acquire just notions of religious duty. The grand means are in the power of every one of you who can read his Bible. In various parts of that all-important volume, but particularly in the New Testament, you will find directions which can scarcely be misunderstood; and which together form that rule of life by which we must be acquitted or condemned at the last great day.—I do not urge you to neglect any kind of reading which has a tendency to cultivate the understanding, to refine the taste and raise it above low sordid pursuits and pleasures, or to cherish the affections which duty approves. There is a time for all things; and those who have leisure to give to such objects, will thus employ it wisely and well. Some portion, however, of that leisure, particularly that which the Lord's day most commonly affords, should be given to the more direct culture of religious principle,—to the acquisition of knowledge respecting God, and our duty to Him, to our fellow-men, and to ourselves,—to the perusal of books which have as their immediate object to impress the grand truth of religion upon the heart, and to cherish in our breasts and strengthen the sense of duty and the devout affections.

But, above all, let me urge you to the thoughtful perusal of some portion of the Scriptures *daily*. I hope you believe that they contain the Revelation of the will of God: and I am sure that those who neglect to give a frequent and sincere attention, to those parts especially which show us the will of God respecting our conduct and dispositions, act the same unwise and hazardous part with the pilot, who, while steering over a dangerous ocean, seldom or never consults his charts and his compass. God has, it is true, placed within us a monitor, which (if we faithfully listen to it) will seldom fail to show us the way that we should go. But this monitor requires to be corrected, strengthened, enlightened, by the Revealed Will of God: and conscience, if duly enlightened, can scarcely fail to show us, that it is our bounden duty to seek for Divine guidance; and to accept gratefully, and to employ sincerely, that which God hath been pleased to bestow. It must be a very proud heart which supposes that it needs not the aid and instruction which the Scriptures afford us.

I do not recommend an indiscriminate perusal of the Scriptures, particularly of the Old Testament. In that daily reading which I would urge upon my young friends, I should wish them to confine themselves to portions of no great length, the direct tendency of which is to cultivate the devout affections, or to enlighten the mind with the knowledge of duty, and impress upon it the awful sanctions of the Gospel: whose direct tendency, in short, is to further the growth of religion in their hearts. If, in reading the Scriptures they would mark such passages, or keep a register of them, they would find it of considerable service. To these I would have them principally confine themselves, when reading for the express purposes of enlightening and invigorating their consciences, and cherishing their devout affections: and on these they should allow their minds to dwell; frequently considering how far their conduct and dispositions agree with the examples and precepts which they contain. Happy are they who, by the wise direction of parents, have had the serious perusing of the Scriptures made an habitual object with them, from their early years;—to whom we can say, as the Apostle could to Timothy, "From a child thou hast known the Holy Scriptures, which are able to make thee wise unto salvation." But, if this has been too much neglected, do not, my young friends, consider it as too late to begin. You may still learn to take delight in the employment; and at any rate you will find it profitable. And, if you pursue it as an object of duty, it will become pleasant; and this in proportion as it does you good.

I am fully persuaded that you cannot proceed long in this employment, without being convinced that half-measures will not do in religion;—that God must have the first place in your hearts, or the world will rule there. I do not call upon you, my young friends, to sacrifice the innocent pleasures and active enjoyments of your period of life. Yours is the season of cheerfulness and activity; and I have no wish to see it gloomy. But I do most earnestly wish, that your pleasures should all be such as will leave no sting behind them; such as you can enjoy with a conscience void of offence. Let pleasure (I here mean innocent pleasure) be pursued only as a subordinate object:—let it never be allowed to engross that time and attention, which are due to the proper duties of your situations in life, or to those objects which are of infinitely higher moment than any present gratification :—and never entertain the idea, that thoughtless, giddy, dissipation is productive of real happiness, any more than it is consistent with duty.

I would therefore urge you from a regard to your happiness as well as to your duty,—

2. That you determine, with the blessing of God, to make it your first and chief concern, to fear, to love, and to obey Him.—Would that we could produce in the mind of any one this determination, so as to fix it there as a steady principle of conduct; for then every thing would be done that our best wishes for you dictate. It is this which is most wanting. Persons are usually less deficient in the knowledge of what is right, than in the steady actuating determination to practice it. I do not say that he who is wavering in his conduct, and sometimes follows the calls of folly or vice, without altogether leaving the guidance of religion, is in the same danger with him who thinks little of religion, and in no degree aims to obey it; but I cannot doubt that he can thus know little of the peace and comfort of religion. Conscience will reprove him more sharply for his neglects of duty, than him who has long slighted her authority and stifled her upbraidings. The time will come when this last also will feel her anguish : but for the present he has less to embitter what he calls his pleasure, than those have who have enough religion to show them that they are doing wrong, and enough tenderness of conscience to punish them for it. As you would wish therefore to obtain the present satis-

factions and peace of religion, *be religious*. Fairly and faithfully make this your aim. Make it your invariable object to live as in the sight of God : and do not let the apprehension of the present reproaches of conscience induce you to slur over your deficiencies and your wanderings. And this leads me to recommend to you strongly,—

3. A frequent, indeed I would say daily, reflection on your conduct. Self-knowledge can only be acquired by self-examination and inspection : and, to discharge this important duty well, it must be done frequently. Indeed the direct duties of religion generally require but little time : and that may in most cases be recovered from sleep. A few minutes spent quietly at the close of the day, in considering how far your temper and conduct during it have been such as they ought to be, in fairly questioning your own hearts as in the sight of God, are minutes well spent ; and, if they are properly improved, will contribute most powerfully to lead you on in the way everlasting. " Judge not that ye be not judged," is an important lesson with respect to others : but, with respect to ourselves, we may reverse the precept, and say " Judge, that ye be not judged." He who goes on without self-examination, can scarcely improve as he ought ; and the probability is that, so far from improving, he will go farther and farther from the mark at which as a Christian he should aim.—An excellent heathen philosopher enjoined upon his disciples, that, before they gave themselves to sleep, they should thrice revolve the actions and events of the day. And here, as in many other instances, the Christian may learn from the heathen. His directions have been thus represented in English by Dr. Watts.—

> "Nor let soft slumber close thine eyes,
>   Ere every action of the day
>   Impartially thou dost survey.
> 'Where have my feet chose out their way?
> 'What have I learnt where'er I've been,
> 'From all I've heard, from all I've seen?
> 'What know I more that's worth the knowing?
> 'What have I done that's worth the doing?
> 'What have I sought that I should shun?
> 'What duties have I left undone?
> 'Or into what new follies run?'
>   These self-enquiries are the road
>   That leads to virtue and to God."

There is a little work, which many have found of uncommon value in assisting them to acquire the knowledge of themselves: I refer to Mason's Self-Knowledge, which I recommend to the serious perusal of those of my young hearers, who have sincerely at heart to know and to do their duty.*

I am sure that no thoughtful person can doubt as to the importance of my

4th Point of advice;—that you exercise great caution in the choice of your companions, (especially of your intimate companions); and that you most carefully avoid all such conversation, and such books, as have a tendency to corrupt the mind, to introduce corrupt thoughts and desires, to make you think less highly of religious duty, to lessen your reverence for virtue, and your abhorrence of vice. Such books, and such conversation, have the most injurious effect on the mind; and, more perhaps than any

---

* A work published since the composition of this Sermon, and for which Dr. C. often expressed a very high value, may be here noticed;—that of the Rev. H. Ware, on the Formation of the Christian Character.——ED.

other cause, pollute the heart, and lead to licentiousness and to wretchedness. It may not be always in your power to avoid hearing language, which even the heathen moralist would condemn: but it is always in your power to avoid joining in it, or in any other way encouraging it. And, if your heart is sincere when you pray "Lead me not into temptation," you will take care not unnecessarily to expose yourselves to it.

I would urge you my young friends,—

5thly,—Carefully to avoid the common error, of forming your notions of duty upon the conduct and expressions of those around you. In any case in which duty is concerned, the question with the Christian never can be, what are the maxims and practice of the world around him; but what are really the directions of the conscience, and of that standard by which we must be acquitted or condemned at the last great day. I do not wish you to set up as rigid censors of others. Circumstances may enable you with propriety, and with effect, to give Christian advice to those around you: but, till experience and stability of character have given influence to your advice, your great object must be to preserve your own consciences void of offence towards God and towards man. By no means aim at singularity. Where duty is not concerned, follow the world. But be careful not to follow it too far. Let it ever be impressed upon your minds, that at the great day of accounts, every one must bear his own burden; that then every one must stand or fall, not by the conduct and character of those around him, but by his own.

To preserve you from the evil that is in the world, I urge you farther,—

6thly,—To cultivate and strengthen in your hearts, by

habitual exercise, the firmness and decision of character, that holy fortitude and resolution of soul, which will arm you against the influence of false shame, and against the temptations which worldly interest or pleasure may present. I have no wish that you should despise the good opinion of those around you. If they are wise and good, their approbation is a treasure; if they have too little regard to wisdom and duty, still their good will has its value; and, where you can have it, without any sacrifice of principle, by kindness and courtesy, gain and enjoy it. But I beseech you to consider that human praise is dearly bought, if purchased by the neglect or breach of duty, by the loss of our peace of mind or of the approbation of God: and that it is infinitely better to bear the temporary pains of ridicule, and worldly censure and disgrace, than to incur the reproaches of conscience, and the displeasure of Almighty God. And, with respect to the temptations which interest or pleasure present, to draw you off from the good old way, be assured that there is only one way to be safe,—that is, to resist them with firmness and steadiness. I would say, too, that there is only one way to be happy; for (as has been well observed by an excellent writer) "it is as impossible for any creature to work out a happiness to itself, in a way contrary to that which its Creator hath appointed, as it is for that creature to make itself anew, or to new-model the whole universe about it." It is an indisputable maxim, that happiness can be securely found, only where God hath placed it; and that He hath placed it in the exercise of uprightness and truth, of temperance and purity, of benevolence and piety.

I fear I have already trespassed on your patience; but

I must not pass by what is among the most essential points,—

7thly,—That, with a view to fulfil your duty from the principles of religious obedience, to check every sinful desire and disposition, to preserve you in the hour of trial, to urge you on in the way that leadeth to life everlasting, and to obtain the favour of Almighty God, you cherish in your hearts an impressive habitual sense of His constant presence and of your accountableness to Him, by steady attention to the means of religion, and, in a particular manner, by private prayer. If you neglect this, there is too much room for apprehension that your goodness will be like the morning cloud or the early dew which soon passeth away. At any rate it cannot be expected that the principle of godliness will grow in your soul, that you will stand firm in the midst of temptation, that, in short, you will live in the fear of the Lord. I therefore urge it upon you, my young friends, with the earnestness of conviction, and of solicitude for your welfare, that you regard it as a duty which you must on no account neglect, to hold daily communion with your Maker in the offering of private prayer. The day begun with serious reflection and prayer, and ended with self-examination and prayer, will most probably be spent as every day should be.—To aid you in this duty, you may usefully employ the assistance of such books as Dr. Toulmin's Manual of Prayers for private devotion, and Mr. Merivale's Devotions for the Closet; and (at an earlier period) Mr. Wellbeloved's Devotional Exercises:—but do not let any thing prevent you from frequently leaving all forms, and devoutly and seriously expressing before Him, who readeth the heart,

Who knoweth our frame, and pitieth them that fear Him, your wants and desires, your feelings of gratitude and of contrition, your purposes of holy obedience, and supplications for those gracious aids which He affords to those who sincerely seek His favour.—The experience of the religious in all ages will bear me out in asserting, that humble earnest prayer, offered by the individual in the sincerity of his heart to his all-seeing Witness and Friend, has, above all other means, the power of producing and strengthening the principle of piety in the soul, and is essential to render all other means effectual. It procures for us strength, guidance, and consolation from the Father of our spirits: and, united with corresponding endeavours to do His will, it will enable you so to live, that, in all circumstances, you may look up with comfort to God as your gracious Father, and may indulge the joyful hope that you will be found among those whom your Lord will own as his, at the last great day.

May the Divine blessing accompany what you have heard; and impress upon your hearts every holy purpose you may form of obedience to His will.

SERMON XI.

ORNAMENTS AND INFLUENCE OF THE FEMALE SEX.

1 PETER III., 3, 4.

WHOSE ADORNING LET IT NOT BE THAT OUTWARD ADORNING OF PLAITING THE HAIR AND OF WEARING OF GOLD, OR OF PUTTING ON OF APPAREL; BUT LET IT BE THE HIDDEN MAN OF THE HEART IN THAT WHICH IS NOT CORRUPTIBLE, EVEN THE ORNAMENT OF A MEEK AND QUIET SPIRIT, WHICH IS IN THE SIGHT OF GOD OF GREAT PRICE.

THE Apostle does not forbid the *outward adorning*; but he urges upon Christian women that this should be *subservient* to the *inward* adorning of the heart.—Our Saviour employs a similar mode of expression, when he says to his disciples (John vi. 27,) "Labour not for the meat which perisheth, but for that meat which endureth unto everlasting life." I believe that, in these and other things (having in themselves no spiritual quality, but depending, for their relation to the welfare of the soul, on the use which is made of them,) the Christian is left at liberty; though required to use that liberty with discretion and moral caution; required carefully to avoid whatever, in kind or degree, is felt to be evil in its effects upon the individual mind,— evil in exciting the working of vanity and self-conceit and contempt for others,—evil in occupying an undue proportion of thought and time,—evil in diverting too much of the pecuniary resources from the channel in which Christian love directs them to flow,—evil in exciting in the minds of others, by an undue stress on outward adornment, that eager desire after it, which may lead them to expenditure, and to the employment of means to defray it, in which uprightness and charity would be alike forgotten.

But such are the doublings and intricacies of the heart, that the greatest simplicity in the adorning of the person may be made, in some, the means of cherishing the same vanity and imagination of superiority, that, in the case of others, are produced by excess of ornament and undue attention to the decoration of the person. No external circumstances can exclude pride from the heart. When the Cynic disdainfully trod over the rich carpet of the highly-gifted disciple of Socrates, and said "Thus I trample on Plato's pride," the reply was as just as it was severe, "Yes, and with much greater pride." It is possible to employ those outward ornaments, which the general custom of the age and nation render suitable to the individual's period of life and station in the social circle, without having the mind set upon them or engrossed by them,—without having its attention diverted from the great purposes of our present existence, or its pursuit of them hindered. It is possible to keep the heart loose to them, while they are employed as others employ them on the outward person. Yet this is one of the trials of the young; and this wise and elevated state of mind, where not early produced by the well-principled wisdom of parental friends, is to be attained only by cultivating right views as to the purposes and duties of life,—by the improvement of the understanding, and by forming a taste for what is solid and useful,—and above all, by cherishing those sentiments and dispositions which respect unseen realities.

Yours, my Young Friends, is the period when the spirit should be cheerful and buoyant. With an ordinary degree of health, you reasonably look forward to maturer age; and even with causes of shortened life, which in the later periods would soon prove too powerful, the great Being by whom we live hath provided sources of restoration and vital energy, which lead us often to say, "there is youth on their side." Nevertheless, on the other hand, settled vigour is not attained; and often the bud of youth has its canker-worm. But supposing life certain, still the morning hours are the preparation for the day. The seed-time is the preparation for the harvest. The morning hours are often bright and joyous;—the spring in its ordinary influences is cheering even to the care-worn heart, its gales are refreshing even to the exhausted spirits;—and to the heart and fancy of inexperienced youth, it is the forerunner of happiness to come, and with it come hope and joyous emotion. But there is a period beyond: and such is the nature of the human mind, that, if all were spring, spring itself would lose much of its power to charm.

The Heavenly Father hath made every thing beautiful in its season, and good for that for which it was designed, if we wisely choose the good and consider the end. We expect not at your period of life, my Young Friends, the matured consideration of the disciplined mind,—disciplined by the trials of life, disciplined by its toils and cares, above all disciplined by the long-continued training of religion. We desire not to see the period of youth prematurely marked by solicitude, or unable to taste the natural enjoyments of life. But we have yet to learn that the dawning light of religion and duty ever made the sun of nature less cheering or invigorating; or that the influence of that faith, which makes the Heavenly Father seen in all His works, renders those works less delightful; or that the considerations of Heavenly wisdom, and the choice of that part which shall never be taken away, render us less able to enjoy the beauties of God's providence in the world around, or lessen the delight in the charities of home and friendship, and in those pleasures which leave no sting behind them.

The religious Instructor, who has the Gospel of Christ as his guide, sees that religion is not intended to prevent the course of Nature or of Providence; but to make it as much as possible, conduct to good, to preserve from what would make us lose sight of our Heavenly destination;—not to take us out of the world, but to guard us from abusing its good things, and to keep us from the evils which are in it. All this requires the exercise of serious thought, and it is well that,—before the fetters of earthly cares, and the engrossing nature of even innocent pursuits, have obtained too fixed a hold upon the mind,—the young should, by the aid of that blessing which they should be early led habitually to seek, cherish that impressive sense of the purposes of life, which shall prevent the formation, or check the growth, of frivolity, and of the eager seeking after outward gratification,—which shall prevent the fearful character being impressed upon them, of being "lovers of pleasure more than the lovers of God."

While, therefore, we slight not the qualities of external gracefulness, and the adorning of the accomplishments, which, in their place and in their degree, may contribute to it,—often connected as this is with health of body, and often promotive of that refinement and delicacy of mind, which are limited to no station in society, and which true religion cherishes, by its sentiments and its spirit;—while the outward adorning, whether of person or manner or acquirement, are not neglected,—let the highest consideration of the Female Young be the incorruptible ornament of the soul within. In the words of the sacred poet, who consecrated his powers to religion, and who hath led many a child of immorality to it,

> " Then let me set my heart to find
> " Inward adorning of the mind ;
> " Knowledge and virtue, truth and grace,—
> " These are the robes of richest dress."

Of this " blest apparel " he says,—

> " It never fades, it ne'er grows old,
> " Nor fears the rain, nor moth, or mould ;
> " It takes no spot, but still refines ;
> " The more 'tis worn, the more it shines."

I do not wish to lead the Female Young to any undue appreciation of themselves individually; or of the station and influence of their sex. But a right estimate of the latter often leads to more correct views of the former; which, by pointing to higher views and aims than those to which female education has too frequently been almost exclusively directed, introduce perhaps lower thoughts of themselves, check the workings of vanity, give a right direction to the love of admiration if it exists, sobers it down into the desire of esteem and approbation, and cherishes, with a sense of duty and the disposition to prepare for its claims, that gentle modesty, which is among the most beautiful ornaments of the female sex, and which never yet, when sterling, was a solitary one.

And here I would particularly address myself to young females, in the character of Daughters and Sisters.—All may not be called to fulfil the duties of Wife and Mother: and I am now particularly addressing those, who are too young to sustain those relations. Here, my Young Friends, your influence and means of service are great. The cheerfulness of youth, when combined with dutiful and watchful love, often enables the Daughter to do much in refreshing the wearied spirit of the Father, worn by the trials of life, irritated by its vexations, and depressed by its disappointments. In such cases, his painful feelings are too much shared by the one who is his fellow-helper, to enable her to smooth his ruffled brow, and to cheer his dejected spirits, so easily as it can be done, with little effort, by the cheerful affection of the well-trained daughter. It may be her blessed privilege to do still more. By making him a partaker of her innocent pleasures, more especially by communicating to him the warm glow of her as yet unchilled Christian benevolence, she may do much in checking that spirit of worldly-mindedness, which is one of the most ensnaring temptations incident to the busy life of manhood.

Nor is the influence of the Sister over the Brother less

valuable. In the Parents he sees those, who, he believes, have outlived that keen sense of pleasure, which Youth possesses; but he knows that the sister can feel it; and, by giving her ready sympathy in all his hopes, and sharing with him his innocent enjoyments, and increasing them by her accomplishments and taste, she may give them a higher relish, and thus materially aid in restraining him from those which are sinful. She may show him by her example, and by the outpouring of her own pure heart and elevated affections, that religion's ways are indeed the ways of pleasantness, that all her paths are peace; and thus cherish in his heart those desires after holy obedience, and that fear of the Lord, which parental care had implanted, and which is indeed the only sure foundation of true wisdom.

The sexes have their respective purposes in life assigned to them by the Lord of all; and for these they are adapted by their respective characteristics of body and of mind. There is even, in the intellectual powers and capabilities, a general distinction: and, without saying how far it is desirable that this should decide the course of education, and how much of the diversity observable may be attributed to education, it is certain that the physical structure of the frame points out, that woman was not designed for the employments of masculine strength, nor to compete in the struggles of public life, nor to engage in those exertions which require a long-continued exercise of bodily vigour. It is certain that the physical texture prepares woman to have most of quickness and sensibility, most gentleness and docility, most patience and meekness, most promptness in judging and vividness of imagination, most sensibility and quickness of fancy; but that it naturally indisposes her, and (unless counteracted by education) in some measure disqualifies her, for that persevering energetic research, that long-continued vigour of application, that intense closeness of investigation, by which the mighty processes of human improvement have been carried on, and by which indeed they have been devised.

Far be it from me to say that, when the female mind, gifted with peculiar powers, and directed in its efforts into a peculiar channel, rises above the pursuits even of the most cultivated part of its sex, and excels even where few men have been able to excel, the possessor of such qualifications should be viewed with other than admiring sentiments;—especially if, as in the case of the one so distinguished in the present day (Mrs. Somerville), her superior powers and attainments are associated with a due attention to the employments of a domestic nature, and adorned with that which is incorruptible,—a meek and modest spirit. But for the great purposes of human life, we would rather see the qualities which have adorned the names of Barbauld and Hamilton, and More and Edgeworth; and the influence of their writings will be much longer experienced, and the character of their minds will much longer live, in the intellectual and moral excellencies which they have produced or fostered in others. *Men* might have done what the most distinguished women in the walks of science have done; but *no man* could have done what Miss Edgeworth and Mrs. Barbauld have in different ways accomplished,—the one for the moral and sound intellectual purposes of this life,—and the other for the training of the soul to a meetness for the life to come.

But all women do not possess the high intellectual

qualifications, of which we have been speaking. Few probably would possess them, even were their powers more judiciously called forth and directed than as yet is common; but all possess those capabilities, and all may possess those qualities, which will, without perhaps making them known beyond the circle of personal agency, give them an influence of the most beneficial kind, in the relations in which they stand to the world around them. All may not be able to write with the glowing characters of imagination; or with the vigour of intellectual strength; or with the persuasive words of comprehensive experience and spiritual wisdom. All cannot possess those brilliant qualities, which often fascinate to delude, and which, however great their power for a time, can endure only for a time.—But the love of truth and kindness may rule the tongue and guide the pen. The sweetness of gentleness, of humility, and of charity, may form the expression of the countenance. The clearness of judgment which religion and conscienciousness give, may be ready at all times to discern the path of sound discretion. The simpleness of purpose which the intimate sense of duty forms, may be continually present to preserve that disinterested uprightness, which is too often lost sight of in the ensnaring transactions of the world. There may always be possessed that devotedness of heart to the purposes of love,—that patient and cheerful self-sacrifice,—that unobtrusive attentive thoughtfulness for others,—that mild compassion,—which continually makes woman the angel of mercy. There may always be in her heart, that abiding operating piety, which, without display, without excitement, perhaps without being perceived out of the circle where the manifestations of it must be discerned, sheds its influence to guide, to strengthen, to soothe, to support, to restrain, and to restore.

Were woman always trained, and could they always train themselves, for such qualifications, what might she not become to human welfare! She would then be prepared for the sacred duties of the mother or maternal friend; or to be in other ways the former and guide of the youthful judgment and affections. She would be prepared to be the companion and the friend of man. She would make his home the dearest place on earth. In early days she would give her influence to the side of virtuous and honourable purpose. She would be the support of every thing excellent in her brothers and their associates; and would aid to raise them above the influence of degrading society, refine their moral taste, elevate their ambition, and aid them to aim at higher applause than that of the worthless. Her influence without observation, (I need not say *without ostentation,* for with it she could have but little,) her influence would promote the estimation of what is truly estimable,—would check the ebullitions of bewildering folly,—would awe the licentious,—would disarm the flattering tongue of its power to poison. When more fully employed in the duties of life, she would be found habitually engaged in the discharge of them, with composure, order, and faithfulness; contributing, in her domestic and friendly connections, to prevent the purposes of benevolence, or of personal interest, from being turned from the course required by wisdom and conscience; promoting the every day comforts of life by discretion and forethought; and, prepared for those great trials and emergencies, in which the fortitude of woman singularly rises, and in which her clear promptness of discernment marks out the direction of safety, whilst her intuitive sense of propriety gives that true dignity which arises from moral fitness; and, when man would sink, she is his effectual support.

I would now address a few brief directions to those who are in the days of preparation.

1. Attend to the health and vigour of the body. Health is important to enable us to discharge well the duties of life. The languor of indisposition is apt to generate the habit of contenting ourselves with the imperfect discharge of duty: and, if such should be our case, we should consider it as one of our leading and constant duties to strive against it, to make it our continual endeavour "that, whatever we do, we shall do it heartily as unto the Lord."—When I recommend you to attend to the health and vigour of the body, I do not wish it to be understood that you should make it your solicitous desire to preserve it;—this would occasion that self-regard, which is inconsistent with the Christian character: but that it should not be risked for any purpose of selfish gratification; and that you should readily follow those directions, which your more experienced friends believe to be desirable, without feeling too solicitous respecting the result.

2. Cultivate the understanding. Every faculty of the human mind should be duly cultivated; and each may be made subservient to this guiding and directing power. The imagination is an essential part of it. When it is under the guidance of right reason, it exalts and elevates and enlarges the mind; and leads it to those more extended views of human duty, which enable the understanding to

see the most desirable ends, and to select the best means of accomplishing them. Nor would I wish to leave out of view the exercise, or the cultivation, of the feelings. Without the feelings, the understanding would often be fruitless; for, without the feelings, we should be cut off from those close and tender sympathies, from whose exercise spring our social duties which, in the early periods of life especially, afford so valuable a culture to the understanding: and, by the exercise of the feelings, the understanding itself is often aided; but it should not be guided by them. The understanding is principally cultivated, and should be guided, by the judgment. In the important duties and decisions of active life, into which females are rarely called, the importance of this valuable faculty is obvious; but it is not less important in the daily routine of domestic duties. Perhaps its exercise is more constantly required to discharge them aright, than in the more mechanical employments of the other sex; but whether that be the case or not, the greater strength of the feelings, the many trying duties of the sick chamber, and of domestic perplexity and sorrow, to which females are called,. render the calm exercise of the judgment of the greatest moment to them.—But the understanding is trained, not only by the cultivation and exercise of the various powers of the mind, but by the faithful discharge of duty, however humble; and particularly by the wise communication, and the faithful and accurate reception of knowledge.*

3. Cultivate the Social Affections, by exercise, and by

* See Dr. Abercrombie's excellent little work on the Culture of the Mind.

avoiding whatever is inconsistent with the most worthy. Carefully regulate and check any taste, any sentiment or affection, which would separate you from those domestic ties, which He who has placed us in families has appointed. The strength of the social affections often gives a true elevation to the female character, which it would not otherwise possess: and often have they been its safeguard; preventing the formation of those attachments which would be subversive of their happiness, or enabling those under their influence to conquer them; or, when they have been rightly placed, smoothing down the difficulties of life, and greatly enhancing its pleasures. In this connection, my Young Friends, let me urge you ever to remember the great importance of carefully guarding the affections, lest they should be placed on any object which duty and religion will not sanction. However much you may imagine that you shall find your happiness in such a one, you may be assured that you will only find bitter disappointment. Happiness can only be found where duty points the way.

4. Cultivate the sense of duty. Enlarge it. It is a broad path, when viewed by the enlightened mind. Enlarge it by knowledge, but seek, too, to enlarge it by exercising it. Exercise it in all your employments,— in the selection of your pleasures. Do always that which is right; and every act, every employment of your time and talents, will be an act of duty, and will strengthen and enlarge your sense of it. God may and will be glorified by all, if all be done "in the name," in the spirit, "of our Lord Jesus Christ." Exercise it in the regulation of your thoughts and desires. Carry it with you into your most retired hours, and into the recesses of

your hearts, into your social intercourse, into your family relations. Let your words be under its influence. Then the law of kindness will guide your social intercourse; while Truth will ever be not only the language of your lips, but the regulator of your thoughts and actions. The young, particularly the female young, have many temptations to deception and evasion, if not to direct falsehood; which are little felt at a more advanced age; and of which the lofty bearing of man knows nothing. Here then, my Young Friends, is one of your greatest dangers. Here is, perhaps, one of the most difficult parts of that warfare, which we are called to exercise against the sins that most easily beset us. Truth is essential to uprightness; and remember that "He" alone "who walketh uprightly walketh surely." Let this ennobling, this essential virtue of the Christian character, be the object of your most careful, most constant, and most earnest cultivation.

5. That we may cultivate this sense of duty, let us be faithful and diligent in the use of the appointed means. Let it be your habitual practice, to read with thoughtful, self-applying, attention, the practical and devotional parts of the Scriptures; and especially to treasure up the instructions of the Lord Jesus, and to impress his character, upon the spirit. Law, in his Essay on Christian Perfection, judiciously remarks that in reading other books, it may be sufficient to know what they contain; but that, when we read the Gospels, our object should be, not merely to know and to treasure up the precepts of our Master, but to imbibe his spirit, that the same mind may be in us which was also in Christ Jesus. In proportion as we are able to do this, in that proportion shall we truly

follow his example, and be transformed into his image; and be fitted for that blessed state, where we shall be like him, for we shall see him as he is.

But we have other means of religious improvement; and let us not slight any of them. Let a part of the leisure of the Lord's day, and, if possible, a part of every day, be spent in that reading which will enlighten the understanding on the subjects of Christian duty, and aid in forming the Christian character. It is well to make extracts from such works; and, if kept for your own reading alone, to subjoin the circumstances of trains of thought which gave them their peculiar value. In making such extracts, do not seek so much for that which excites the feelings, or captivates the imagination, as for the practical directions of experienced Christians. There is another means of training the mind to habits of serious thought and self-examination, which, however, I would recommend with caution; this is making memoranda of the results of our self-examinations. This, if care be not taken, may be made only the means of self-deception; but, if pursued with thoughtful care, and simplicity of intention, will be an important means of acquiring the most valuable of all knowledge,—the knowledge of ourselves.

6. Cultivate, in a more particular manner, the sentiments and the feelings of piety, and the habit of devotion. Piety towards God is the most ennobling sentiment of the mind;—our greatest, and sometimes our only safeguard in the moral dangers which surround us:—our unfailing support in the sorrows and trials of life,—and the source of our greatest and purest happiness. But this plant of "heavenly mould" needs careful cultivation. Every-

thing which sullies the purity of our souls prevents its formation and exercise; and it requires to be constantly fostered by all those influences by which the religious affections can be cherished, and particularly by habitual prayer, as well as by the constant influence of a devotional temper. Live continually as seeing Him who is invisible. In all your pursuits and innocent recreations, keep the end of all in view; and, however beneficial the pleasures and advantages of life may appear, and may really be in their place and degree, remember that "one thing is needful." And may it be said of each of you, as of Mary, that you have "chosen that good part which shall never be taken away."

SERMON XII.

HOPE IN GOD.

PSALM XLII., 11.

WHY ART THOU CAST DOWN, O MY SOUL? AND WHY ART THOU DISQUIETED WITHIN ME? HOPE THOU IN GOD!

PECULIAR must have been the circumstances of the good man, who has not had occasion to resort to the tranquil comforts of religion,—who has not known what it is to sorrow at *present* distress, or to feel the emotions of solicitude and apprehension at the prospect of *future* calamity. Perhaps, too, there are few whose hearts are open to its consoling efficacy, that have not experienced the soothing and peaceful influence of the words of the pious Psalmist. It is indeed a great happiness, when, by the early care of religious parents and friends, the mind has been led to treasure up the devotional sentiments of the Scriptures, and to employ them in the periods of holy meditation and prayer. They thus become familiar, and often recur with readiness when the head is unable to pursue any long train of reasoning, and the heart seems incapable of rising from the pressure of present or expected evils; and they have, in innumerable instances, been the means of diffusing peace and hope and consolation.

The verse which I have selected for my text, occurs

(with a little variation) twice in the 42nd Psalm, and again at the end of the 43rd. It has been conjectured, and not without considerable probability, that these two Psalms were once in one. At any rate they must have been composed by the same author, nearly at the same time, and in the same circumstances. There appears little room to hesitate in receiving these Psalms as the compositions of David, during the period when he was obliged to wander in the desolate and secluded parts of the country, in order to avoid the envious fury of Saul, or the unnatural conspiracy of the rebellious Absalom. Unable to share in the public services of religion, in which this servant of God manifested great delight; a destitute fugitive, and often exposed to danger from the cruel purposes of his enemies,—it is not surprising that his heart sometimes sunk with him. He might perceive no termination to his calamities, and might reasonably apprehend that, if he were not at last a prey to those who sought his life, he should still be a wanderer, "houseless, sole, forlorn," destitute of the comforts of a settled home, continually full of alarm, deprived of the alleviations of friendly solicitude and sympathy, and (what he seems to have felt more than all) unable any longer to go to the House of God with the voice of joy and praise;—and in such circumstances, his mind must have been possessed of singular fortitude, or I should rather say of singular apathy, if it did not often experience distress, and sometimes perhaps despondency. The waves and billows of affliction rolled over him; and disquieting thoughts and gloomy forebodings must sometimes have intercepted the gentle current ever flowing from the fountain of Divine mercy.

How interesting to think of the pious Psalmist, in such an hour of darkness, resisting the encroaching feelings of gloom and despair, and checking their progress; and, by the exercise of humble but steadfast reliance upon God, rising above their influence, and looking forward to days of light and comfort. "Great indeed are my present afflictions, (we may conceive him to say), sorrows seem to dwell around me, and to hide the future in darkness and distress;—but why art thou cast down, O my soul, and why art thou disquieted within me? Hope thou in God, for thou shalt yet praise Him, as thy deliverer from evil, as well as thy God." Little did the Psalmist think, when he committed to writing these sentiments of devotional solitude, that they would communicate to thousands and tens of thousands in after ages, that tranquillizing influence which he himself experienced from them. But they have been preserved by the hand of Providence; and they are among the means by which the great Father of spirits directs the principles of those who sincerely and habitually acknowledge Him. When their course lies through the vale of tears, as well as when they have to contend with moral difficulties and dangers, His word is indeed a lamp to their feet, and a light unto their paths. It guides them through the wilderness like the pillar of cloud by day, and the pillar of fire by night.

Without hope, wretched indeed would be the condition of man. Even when the sun of prosperity is without a cloud, if there were no hope for the future, the heart could not long receive its enlivening beams. But such is the nature of that wonderful principle, which the Author of our frame has placed within us, by which He has enabled us to retrace the past, and look forward to the future, that peculiar indeed must be the circumstances of him whose breast hope has deserted. Leaving out of view those cases where bodily distress destroys the spring and activity of the mind, hope can only be expelled by sensuality, by irreligion, or by those gloomy notions of Him who is love, which involve His character and ways in more than Egyptian darkness,—darkness that may be felt, and often has been felt, to the utter exclusion of light and peace.

Hope, by its own natural buoyancy, often raises the minds even of those who live without God in the world, above the influence of present disappointments and anxieties. But my immediate object is Hope in God. Religious principle gives a stability and value to hope, which, without it, hope can never possess. It may sometimes sober down its gay pageantry; but it presents it with a firmer basis upon which it may rest with solid satisfaction. Religion not only encourages us, but it bids us to hope; and it tells us to place our hope on Him who never forsook the heart sincerely devoted to His fear. It tells us to place our hope on Him who hath been a refuge to the good through all generations. It bids us rest on the Rock of ages.

And can this be otherwise than a firm basis for confiding hope?—for hope full of consolation? Not indeed for the ecstacies of Enthusiasm, (who fancies that she sees the all-wise Disposer of all events continually interfering to supply her wants, and to remove her distresses, by means which would be utterly inconsistent with the grand moral order of His providence,)—not indeed for the ecstacies of enthusiasm, but for what is far better,—for the cheering elevating conviction, that *all* is under the wisest and the best direction, and that a period will come when those who attain the great end of their faith and hope, will fully see with admiring gratitude (what now they see in part) that the steps of the good man are indeed ordered by the Lord, and that He conducteth him by the right way to His heavenly kingdom. That the Providence of God is absolutely universal, and comprehends all times, all places, and all events;—that all His purposes are prompted by infinite goodness;—that they are all guided by infinite wisdom;—and that He who ruleth over all has almighty power to accomplish all His wise and gracious designs;—these are the solid foundations, on which the religious mind may rest its hope with gratitude and confidence. And those who spake by the express authority of God have left us no room to doubt. They assure us that "of Him and by Him, and unto Him are all things;" they teach us that nothing is without Him; —that not even a sparrow falleth to the ground without our Heavenly Father;—that He not only ruleth among the nations, but so orders the events of life, that all things work together for good to those who love Him. The doctrine of a universal Providence includes the Scriptural doctrine of a particular Providence; and, though it gives the good man no ground to expect any *miraculous* interpositions of Divine power, to heal his diseases, to supply his wants, to avert his dangers, to remove the load which presses heavily upon his spirits, to dissipate the threatening storm,—yet it does afford solid ground for the conviction, that even his afflictions may promote his highest interests,—that it is a part of the established order of God's moral government, that it shall be well with those who fear Him,—and that, to those who seek His favour by obedience to His will, who maintain habitual communion with Him, and who suitably apply to the Throne of Grace, those supplies of guidance, of strength, and of comfort, will be given, (in ways perhaps which we can scarcely understand, but which are real and effectual,) which enable the Christian traveller to pursue his journey heavenward, with general tranquillity, with comfort and with peace.

Where religious principle fully operates, and is aided in its influence by health of body and natural composure of mind, the disquieting and depressing emotions of the heart less highly favoured are perhaps but little known. Yet it is very seldom that a long period passes to any, without some interval of darkness; and then is the time to call into exercise those encouraging and animating principles, which it is alike our duty and our privilege to cherish and employ.—" Why art thou cast down, O my soul, and why art thou disquieted within me?" Does thy dejection spring from the consciousness of great imperfection in thy religious character, of wrong habits not yet subdued, of wrong dispositions too often exercised, of "talents wasted, time mis-spent?"—dost thou feel apprehensive lest thou shouldst fail of reaching the promised inheritance?—dost thou lament thy limited usefulness, thy inability to accomplish the purposes which thy benevolence prompts thee to form?—dost thou mourn for good resolutions often formed, but which have vanished like the morning cloud or the early dew?—dost thou reflect with distress on negligence in the work assigned thee; or impatience under the afflictions with which thy Father has visited thee, on the little progress which thou hast made in the subjecting thy desires and dispositions to the law of God?—dost thou fear lest thy fortitude should be unable to resist the temptations and the difficulties which surround thee, or lest thy principles should prove too weak to withstand the constant influence of present interests and cares and pleasures, which tend to check or stop thee on thy progress heavenward? Certainly thou hast room for caution, but not for despair. Blessed are they who mourn, with godly sorrow, for they shall be comforted. Do not forget that thou art in the hands of a wise and gracious Parent, who knoweth our frame, who remembereth that we are but dust; that as a father pitieth his children, so the Lord pitieth them that fear Him.—Our unallowed defects and imperfections should indeed render us watchful and humble; but they should not exclude the cheering rays of Divine mercy. The promises of the Gospel, while they afford no hope to the impenitent and disobedient, do give the best consolation to the weary and heavy-laden. We cannot doubt the mercy of God; for it rests on His own gracious declaration. His sacrifices are a broken spirit; and most assuredly a broken and a contrite heart, He will not despise. Despair?—The Christian despair, who possesses the Covenant of love and mercy made through Jesus Christ?—It should not be. Go Christian, who mournest for thy spiritual disorders; and, in the hour of holy retirement, lay open thy heart, with all its wants and weaknesses, before Him who can read the language of the silent tear, who needs not the aid of words to understand thy silent aspirations after obedience to His will, after the spirit of him who hath trodden before us in the path of holy obedience. He who in ways, which perhaps we cannot fully understand, communicates His gracious aid to those who humbly and steadily seek His favour, will answer thy habitual supplications with strength in temptation, and with guidance in moral perplexities, such as they cannot know, who, through high ideas of their own firmness and strength of principle, restrain prayer before God, and neglect the Rock of their salvation. Why, then, art thou cast down, O my soul, and why art thou disquieted within me? Hope thou in God, the God of grace and of all consolation, the Almighty Guardian of those who love and fear Him, the gracious Being who will make it well with them here and well with them for ever. Seek His favour and His gracious succour, with full purpose of heart. Sink not under difficulties; but lean on His powerful arm. Be sober and watch unto prayer; and then thy end will be full of peace and hope. Or if, through some unhappy habits of mind, thou canst not rise from the valley of humiliation, and darkness accompany thee unto the end, a day will come which shall be without a cloud to interrupt the light of Gospel mercy. Certainly it is not the Christian's duty to dwell in desponding sorrow; and there must be some wrong principles within, which cause and continue it. But even such sorrow is better than the wild and destructive mirth of riot and excess; and "blessed is the man that feareth always." "He that goeth forth and weepeth, bearing precious seed, shall doubtless come again with rejoicing, bearing his sheaves with him."

But do your disquietude and despondency arise from feelings of distrust in the goodness of God? The momentary feeling may exist, without leaving a moral stain behind it; but assuredly it cannot habitually exist, without great culpability. Instances, I believe, have been known, (I think I have myself known one), where the fear of God ruled in the heart, where the individual would on no account have *done* any thing inconsistent with the Divine commandments, where nevertheless (from excess of sensibility to the sufferings of others, and early incorrect ideas as to the Divine dispensations, and the influence of bodily weakness disposing the mind to dwell upon what was painful instead of what was cheering,) there have been too frequently, nay almost habitually, in the mind, disquieting distressing apprehensions as to the goodness of Him who is love, which have thrown a gloom over His works, and over His dealings with mankind. He who alone knoweth all the silent movements of the heart, and sees "when frailty errs and when we sin," can appreciate the moral culpability of such distrust; and doubtless He will make all reasonable allowances for human ignorance and imperfection. But certainly we ought never to permit ourselves to cherish those views which lead to it, or harbour it when it does for a moment enter the mind. Distrust as to the goodness of God is indeed enough to make the heart gloomy, and to cause disquietude and despondency. Certainly we do see what we cannot here account for. We see suffering; and, what is a still greater difficulty, we see moral evil: and how all this is consistent with the Infinite goodness of God, we do not comprehend,—perhaps we cannot comprehend. One end *we do know*; that suffering and evil are inseparably connected with this life, considered as a state of probation; and that one grand purpose of them is accomplished, when they lead man to seek to promote the welfare and spiritual improvement of his fellow-man, to desire and endeavour to promote them at the expense of his own gratifications of ease and interest, to cultivate trust and confiding submission to the disposals of Infinite wisdom, to raise his affections towards that state where we shall see face to face, and know even as we are known. But he who is favoured with the light of Revelation, who there sees that God is acquainted with the minutest event, and takes care of the meanest of His creatures, he who has thereby learnt to read the book of Nature, and see there inscribed in characters which he who runs may read, that the Lord is good unto all, and that His tender mercies are over all His works,—*he* has no ground which the understanding can approve, to doubt or to distrust the goodness which prompts Infinite power and wisdom. But, why art thou cast down, O my soul, and why art thou disquieted within me?—may he say, when he contemplates the disorders which, within his own narrow sphere of personal observation, and in the wider circle of states and nations, arise from the operation of the laws of nature, or still more from the evil passions of men. Hope thou in God. He is good; for millions of beings, and millions of millions, beyond the power of the human understanding to reckon up, even in this world, have been called into existence by His gracious power, have received from Infinite wisdom an exquisite structure suited to their several wants and capacities of enjoyment, and all are continually under the care of His bounty, continually supported by His hand. And this world is only a speck of His creation. There are in the boundless fields of space, worlds beyond worlds, and systems beyond systems, all the work of His hand, supported by His constant agency, preserved in order and harmony by His wise superintendence, and all of them (we cannot doubt it) the residence of beings capable, like those which inhabit this earth, of happiness, and receiving it in their due measures and degrees from the Hand that sustains all, from the never-failing stores of that boundless Love which is diffused in copious streams throughout the whole creation. And if the heart, thoughtfully contemplating the wonders of nature, and the rich displays which are there afforded of the goodness of the great Creator, the constant Supporter and Preserver of all, still cannot rise above the influence of the present calamity and evil, let it extend its view to that state which Christianity discloses to the eye of faith, to that life and immortality which Jesus hath brought to light through the Gospel. Let the pious Christian, disquieted at the marks of sin and sorrow, here look forward to those great things which are reserved for those who truly love God. Let him remember, that there is another and a better world; a world where sin and sorrow shall be known no more for ever, where every tear shall be wiped from every eye, and where all shall be advancing in holiness and happiness through the countless ages of eternity. Let him indulge the assured expectation, that all which here is known but in part, will there be fully known; that the time will come when all enemies shall be subdued; and when God shall be all in all.

And to the same prospects let us resort, when our hearts sink within us under the pressure of present calamity, or in the apprehension of future evils. Still "why art thou cast down, O my soul, and why art thou disquieted within me?" Still, hope in God.—Affliction thou shouldst regard as the chastisement of a wise Parent, fitted to improve thy best dispositions, to purify thy desires, and to promote thy progress in those qualities of heart and life, which will render thee a fit object of the Divine mercy and acceptance. Certainly no afflictions can for the present be otherwise than grievous. Yet every one must proceed from the hand of God; and we may indulge the fullest confidence, that our afflictions will last no longer, nor be more severe, than is necessary to accomplish the purposes of a Father's love. Religion teaches us to entertain the firm conviction, that those whose hearts are, in the midst of much weakness and imperfection, really devoted to the fear and love of God, are the objects of His special favour and regard. And if we have a comfortable hope that we are in that blessed number, we may rely with the fullest confidence on the assurances of the Volume of grace, that all things will work together for our good.

But perhaps the heart of those, who not only know present difficulties and distresses, but whom circumstances peculiar to themselves, or such as are common to these times of perhaps unexampled distress (1815) force to view the future with apprehension, may be disposed to reply,— "In affliction, merely respecting ourselves, or such as can be alleviated, we can entertain and cherish trust and resignation; but hope is difficult when there is no apparent ground for hope;—when darkness and solicitude, general and deeply felt, are round about us, and no human eye can discern the means of deliverence from the apprehended calamity." I admit, I feel the appeal; yet still into the religious heart, I trust the words of the Psalmist will introduce some rays of comfort. The promises of God to those who truly seek his favour with full purpose of heart, are not few; and the experience of the pious mind in all ages, proves that they are "yea and amen." "Cast thy burden on the Lord, and He shall sustain thee." Look back upon the days that are past. Have you never found that gloom, thickening gloom, as it appeared, has been dissipated? Have you never perceived the way of Providence become clear and bright, when before it was covered, to your imagination, with mist and darkness? In the course of Nature, do days of darkness continue for ever? Does not the sunshine follow the storm? And is it not alike the case in the moral Providence of God? Wait then patiently upon the Lord. Seek with humble perseverance, for the peace of those whose mind is stayed upon God: and trust that, in His own good time, the darkness which now hangs over thy lot, and the lot of myriads of thy countrymen, will be dispersed. Who is there among you that feareth the Lord?—that walketh in darkness, and hath no light? Let him trust in the name of the Lord, and stay upon his God. If the present sources of industry are dried up, if those who would gladly rise up early and sit up late, only to gain the bread of sorrow, have now the painful feeling that their hands cannot obtain the necessaries of life, for themselves and for those who depend upon them,—let them not add to their solicitude the distresses of distrust and despair. Sufficient for the day is the evil thereof. Let them watch the openings of Providence with humble faith in Him who doeth all things well. Let them employ all prudent means to obtain relief for their distresses. Above all, let no distrust, no anxiety, lead them to break the commandments of God, or seek for succour by means which they cannot beg of God to prosper. And in the moments of despondency, let this be the language of their hearts, " Why art thou cast down O my soul, and why art thou disquieted within me ? Hope thou in God."

Here I will conclude, in the language of the Apostle, " Be careful (anxiously careful) for nothing; but in every thing, by prayer and supplication with thanksgiving, let your requests be made known unto God; and may the peace of God, which passeth all understanding, keep your hearts and minds, through Christ Jesus." Amen.

SERMON XIII.

THE CLOUD NOT BIGGER THAN A MAN'S HAND.

1 KINGS, XVIII., 44.

AND IT CAME TO PASS AT THE SEVENTH TIME, THAT HE SAID, BEHOLD THERE ARISETH A LITTLE CLOUD OUT OF THE SEA LIKE A MAN'S HAND. AND HE SAID GO UP, SAY UNTO AHAB, PREPARE THY CHARIOT, AND GET THEE DOWN, THAT THE RAIN STOP THEE NOT.

THERE are few portions of the history of the servants of the Lord among the children of Israel, more full of animating encouragement to trust in God, and to the exercise of that moral courage which a sense of duty inspires, than this of Elijah. Ahab, son of Omri, exceeded in wickedness all that had preceded him on the throne of Israel; and, as if it had been a light matter to walk in the sinful steps of Jeroboam, who led Israel into idolatry, he married Jezebel the daughter of the King of Sidon, and went and served Baal, and built an altar in a temple to that Idol, and prepared a grove for its abominable rites. The prophet of Jehovah, in the name of the great Being whom he faithfully served, declared to the idolatrous King of Israel, that for three years there should be no dew nor rain in the land, but according to his word. It was by the word of Him who hath all the powers of nature under

His control, that the prophet spake. The dew and the rain came not to the thirsty land; and among the inhabitants of it there must have been sore distress; though probably in the palace of the King there were the usual scenes of luxury and self-indulgence. The heart of man is hardened by sinful pleasure, and by worshipping the idols of the world. The prophet himself was supported by the miraculous sustenance granted to the widow of Sarepta; who in her own extremity, had faith in God, and supplied the wants of the servant whom He had sent to her abode. In the providence of God, self-denying exertions, and sacrifices for the welfare of others, rarely fail to experience (though perhaps at a distant period) some unlooked-for requital,—impressively rewarding, when the exertion, or the sacrifice, had simply in view the dictates of duty and of love.

The third year came to the suffering people, and the appointed time arrived for the manifestation of Jehovah's mercy. The prophet was sent to show himself unto Ahab, preparatory to the renewal of rain from heaven. Doubtless in every part of his subsequent course, he was specially directed by God; but his faith and courage were put to a severe trial. *We* know the result; but to Elijah all was future. The miraculous suspension of rain after his prediction, the miracles he had himself witnessed and shared, precluded the possibility of his being mistaken as to the source of his mission; the principle of obedience was in his heart; and the will of Jehovah, however it was made known to him, was sure to be his guide. The composure and steadfastness with which he followed that guidance, with the circumstances attending the sacrifice on Mount Carmel, excite emotions of moral sublimity, which are comparable in intensity and interest with the hour when Abraham *offered*, though he did not *sacrifice*, his son to the Great Being who gave him as the heir of promise,—or that when the fiery furnace awaited the three servants who would not bow to the golden image,— or that when the blessed prophet prayed, with open window, and his face turned towards Jerusalem, as aforetime, though the den of lions was prepared for him that disobeyed the rash decree of the Persian monarch.

If you ask, whence sprang the elevating, confiding, conviction so vividly manifested by these servants of the Lord, the answer is plain; it was from faith in God, written in their hearts as it may be written in ours, operating habitually as a principle of conduct, leading to obedience in danger and in difficulty, to trust in darkness, to follow the Divine goodness when it was leading they knew not whither, to make duty their paramount consideration; it was that principle which *he* manifested in its most complete and perfect form, who is preeminently the Christian pattern and guide, who could say "My meat is to do the will of my Father, and to finish His work," "I seek not mine own glory but the glory of Him that sent me."—who overcame the world and all its terrors,— and who said, in the hour of sore anguish and agony of spirit, when without all was darkness, and no streak of light appeared in the distant horizon, "Father, not my will but Thine be done."

In the case of the holy Prophet of Israel, we see developed the secret spring of his conduct, in the scenes of that memorable day when the Priests of Baal in full array were assembled on the summit of Carmel, where there was no covering but the vault of heaven, no cloud to interrupt the intense rays of that glorious creature whom they worshipped instead of his Creator, no hidden resources (as in the temple or the grove) for the exercise of mysteries and imposture. The vast plain of Israel once filled with fertility, now barren with the drought, was in full view on the East; and on the West was the majestic Ocean. What was more fitted to raise the soul in humble adoring reverence to Jehovah, the Almighty maker of heaven and of earth? And there, as on Mount Sinai, He manifested His presence and His will; formerly to give laws to His chosen people; and now to recall them to their allegiance. The Priests of Baal uttered their wild invocations from morning unto noon, and cut themselves after their manner with knives and lancets; and they continued their cries and their self-inflictions till the time of the offering of the evening sacrifice. But there was neither voice, nor any to answer, nor any that regarded. And then arrived the period for the solemn appeal to Jehovah. The Prophet with calm dignity, and with deliberate course, (pursued in the sight of assembled Israel), had, in the way of preparation, taken twelve stones as the symbols of the twelve tribes of Israel, and renewed the altar of Jehovah, and dug a trench around it, and put in order the wood for the burnt offering, and placed the bullock in pieces upon it, and the second, and again the third time commanded to pour abundance of water over the wood and the sacrifice till even the trench was filled with water. All was now ready, and doubtless every eye was fixed, and every heart filled with anxious suspense; but there was one heart in which there was no anxiety, which was then filled with earnest faith and solemn expectation. "And it came to pass (saith the sacred record) at the time of the offering of the evening sacrifice, that Elijah the prophet came near, and said, 'Lord God of Abraham, Isaac, and of Israel, let it be known this day that Thou art God in Israel, and that I am Thy servant, and that I have done all these things at Thy word.'"

You know the issue. The fire of Jehovah fell, and consumed the burnt sacrifice, and the wood and the stones and the dust, and dried up the water in the trench. What unbelief could resist the appeal? The people, when they saw it, fell on their faces, and uttered their conviction that Jehovah is God and He alone. The Prophet then foretold to Ahab the approach of abundant rain; but as yet there was no sign of it in the heavens. He then returned to the Promontory of Mount Carmel, and in earnest (and now perhaps anxious) expectation he seated himself on the ground, with his face between his knees, awaiting the fulfilment of the word which he had spoken by the order of the Lord. He goes not himself to look for the signs of its approach; but sends his servant to the point of observation; and the answer is, "there is nothing."

Elijah (saith the Apostle of Christ) was a man subject to like passions with ourselves; and how true to nature the picture of the historian is, let those say, who have seen some great event on the eve of its accomplishment, on which depends the welfare of millions, and the fulfilment of hopes on which the heart had dwelt for years, and to which all the energies of the soul had been directed,—who have watched the signs of the times, and, as they believed, saw the appointed moment at hand,—who have awaited in breathless suspense the looked-for intelligence for good or for ill, but who dare not go themselves to learn the issue, and awaited in silence and solitude the arrival of some less earnest messenger, dispatched to know what had come to pass.

God tries his servants in different ways. At the end of the dispensation of the Law and the Prophets, there was a period of darkness over the whole land for three hours; when human hope seemed fled for ever,—and it rested only in *his* heart, who saw in the gloom itself the proofs of his Heavenly Father's love and approbation, the proof that those great purposes for which he was suffering all that the mortal frame can suffer, and was just about to enter the abode of death, would be accomplished by His mighty power, and he himself be made the author of eternal salvation, and become the Redeemer of the world. *Here* was a period when all was excess of brightness, when the servant of Jehovah earnestly desired that the thick clouds should spread over the firmament, and pour forth torrents to renew the verdure of the earth, and provide food for man and for beast, and lead the whole land of Israel to acknowledge His power, and adore His justice and His mercy. The servant of Elijah returned again and again at his master's command, till the seventh time. "And it came to pass at the seventh time that he said, 'Behold there ariseth a little cloud out of the sea, like a man's hand.'" Suspense is at an end. The Prophet's heart is filled with solemn, earnest, joyful emotion. He sends the message to Ahab, announcing the fulfilment of the heavenly promise; and before it reached the King of Israel, the heaven was black with clouds and wind, and "there was a great rain."

There are those whom neither the judgments nor the mercies of God can affect. The idolatrous Jezebel thought only of vengeance for the destruction of the priests of her deity; and she sought to slay the prophet of Jehovah. Too probably, also, many—even those who witnessed the wonders on Mount Carmel—again bowed the knee unto Baal. Our own experience, perhaps, though in a less fearful way, may teach us the nature of their backsliding. They owned Jehovah as their God; they uttered His praise; but they soon forgot His works. Nevertheless, when the poor prophet, in the solitudes of Horeb, whither he had fled for refuge (after the hour of despondency which followed the period of intense and elevated exertion and holy faith), seemed to himself *alone in the world*, the word of the Lord declared, "I have left me seven thousand in Israel, which have not bowed the knee unto Baal, or adored him with the lips."

The history which we have been considering is so full of impressive instruction and dutiful influence, and so calculated to cherish a trustful faith in the Almighty, in His providence, and in the purposes of His dispensation, that (without further observation made now or hereafter,) I should feel that our time had been well spent, in proportion as the attention, the considerate reflective attention, of my hearers, has been directed to it. HAVE FAITH IN GOD, AND DO YOUR DUTY, is the lesson to all; we all must feel the influence of the Prophet's fortitude, and steadfastness, and perseverance, founded on the convictions of duty, and on the deep-seated and habitual regard to God, which his life displays, and which are manifested in the trying circumstances which have come before us. And those who have had much experience in life, and observed the great revolutions and changes in the world around them, can scarcely avoid also reflections, full of deep and grateful interest, at the events which have been passing in this generation, and which have, (in various ways, and often when all was clouds and darkness,) been so contributing to the great purposes of human welfare and improvement, that even he that despaired for his race, when forty years ago he contemplated the devastation of the moral volcano, or subsequently the gigantic power of ambition carrying along with it the sword and the flames, can have now no reason to doubt (however much he may still see of evil) that the reign of knowledge and liberty and peace and righteousness is advancing, that the dominion of Christ is extending, and that there is nothing in the nature or circumstances of man, which should prevent the fulfilment of that heart-inspiring declaration, "The knowledge of Jehovah shall cover the earth as the waters do the channels of the deep,"—nothing to prevent the final, however distant, accomplishment of the prayer, which the faithful dutiful heart never breathed in vain, "Thy will be done on earth, as it is done in heaven."

"My people do not consider," was the word of the Lord by Isaiah; and, hurried along as we have been by the stream of events, it may be that some of us can fully enter into the force of an expression which came lately from the pen of a distinguished labourer in one important field of benevolent service,—"*when we have leisure for it*, I hope we shall be very thankful." The time of comparative leisure is come, when it is well to review our mercies, and consider our duties. The cloud not bigger than a man's hand, for which many of us watched more than seven times in vain, has showed itself, and is expanding; full, as we may reasonably believe, of blessings to the human race. It may indeed pour forth its torrents, as well as its genial showers. It may still burst in thunders, as well as in calm refreshing influences. But, after all we have seen with our own eyes (or heard, the younger among us, from our fathers) of the dealing of Providence, and of the way in which evil tends to good, and of the indications of the truth that evil has its tendency to extermination, and shall extend no further and last no longer than is needed, in the unsearchable counsels of infinite Wisdom and almighty Power, to accomplish the purposes of boundless Goodness,—who is there that, when contemplating the world with the eye which has been directed upwards to the Throne of grace, and onwards towards eternity, can hesitate to believe that of Him and through Him and to Him are all things, and to join in the song of heaven, Hallelujah, the Lord God Omnipotent reigneth. Blessed are those who in the world around, and in the world within, employ their talents and opportunities to carry on the great purposes of Divine love,—to make others, and to be themselves, as the children of God, the servants of Christ, the brethren of one family here, and expectants of one heavenly home.

My thoughts have been particularly led to the subject to which I have endeavoured to direct yours, by the recent death of one whose name was, from childhood to early manhood, familiar to one's lips, and whom I have always revered as a benefactor to mankind under the highest and noblest influences,—I mean Mr. Wilberforce. I had the opportunity, which I embraced with earnestness, of uniting in the solemn respect paid to his memory at his funeral; and looking back at the period when his services for human welfare began, and at the still more remote period, when the cloud was not bigger than a man's hand and scarcely discernable, when that individual* began to labour

* Thomas Clarkson.

with self-devotement, and with an earnest perseverance which nothing but a sense of duty could have inspired, who still lives to observe the results, while the distinguished advocate of the same cause in the British Senate has had his dismissal, at the time that the great purpose of his life was clearly on the verge of accomplishment,—and perceiving, in rapid retrospect, how the great work of wisdom and justice and benevolence has been advancing, often like the unnoticed swelling of the water in the retired cavern, till at last it has been put in train for full operation, on principles in which (as I know) equity to all, and the welfare of those for whom we were bound to make exertions and sacrifices, have been united beyond all previous hope and expectation,—I feel that the claims of gratitude for this and other national mercies are very strong;—and I wish to lead your heart and hope, through the contemplation of them, to increased faith and trust in the Almighty Father of all, and to increased zeal and perseverance in every good work,—in an increased degree to the patience of hope and the labour of love.

SERMON XIV.

THE CHRISTIAN'S PEACE.

JOHN XIV., 27.

PEACE I LEAVE WITH YOU; MY PEACE I GIVE UNTO YOU; NOT AS THE WORLD GIVETH, GIVE I UNTO YOU.

These words form a part of that deeply interesting discourse, which our Lord addressed to the eleven disciples, just before he retired to the spot where he was to be delivered up to the malice of his enemies; and they must for the time have produced in their minds that soothing tranquillity, with which the perusal of them is usually attended, when the heart has been in some good measure brought into subjection to the principles of the Gospel.

They have an obvious and direct reference to the common form of salutation among the easterns,—" Peace be unto you:" and, explained by this allusion alone, they are affecting. "You have my best desires for your welfare. The world around you often expressed the same wishes, but too often insincerely, or at least thoughtlessly. Mine arise from the most affectionate concern for you." But I cannot persuade myself that this is all which is implied in the words of my text. They appear to me to have a much stronger and more important force. Considering our Lord, not merely in the light of a common friend, but also as one who came to communicate to mankind the glad tidings of Salvation;—considering the situation in which he stood, not merely as about to be separated from those who had personally known him, and whom he loved with no ordinary affection, but also as about to seal by his blood the covenant of grace and mercy,—I apprehend that these expressions may be thus understood, "I leave you, but I leave you not destitute. Peace I leave with you; my peace I give unto you. I give you the means of securing that peace which arises from an interest in the blessings I come to bring to mankind. The world promises happiness; but the sources which it presents to you are unproductive and insecure. I give, not as the world giveth; I present to you that whose value the world cannot understand, which the world cannot bestow, and of which the world cannot deprive you; that peace which I feel; and of which you will partake, by following me in the paths of obedience to the will of my Father."

In the most important sense, godliness hath the promise of the life that now is, as well as of that which is to come. Taking life throughout all its changes, (and how changeful it is, experience is daily teaching us,) there cannot be a doubt that the man who submits his conduct and dispositions to the rules of religion, will possess the greatest share of happiness even in this life. As a general rule it may be most correctly asserted, that he will obtain the fullest share of enjoyment which wisdom, if guided by no prospect of an hereafter, would point as the most rational object of pursuit. But if we advance further, and view the present state, as the Gospel teaches us to view it, as only the infancy of our being, and see religion blending, with present sources of joy and sorrow, its own hopes and fears,—the most sceptical must be forced to allow, that its ways are alone the ways of pleasantness, that its paths are peace. It must indeed be admitted, that the completely irreligious man draws more pleasure from the practice of sin, than he can do who has ever had an operating conviction of the omnipresence of God, and of the certainty of a day of righteous retribution. But for that pleasure he gives up satisfactions, which would themselves abundantly compensate for the loss of any present gratifications; he gives up too his hopes of happiness, compared with which all joys that have no title to the heart are trivial in the extreme.

The present happiness which usually arises from that due regulation of the heart and life which the Gospel enjoins, is well denominated *peace*. There generally are, indeed, periods in the Christian's life, which may in the strictest sense be termed joyful,—such as set at nought every thing which the world calls pleasure, such as furnish a foretaste of that happiness which is laid up for those who love God. But it does not appear that the acquisition of *present* happiness, even of the purest and most valuable kind, is the object of this life;—it is rather the acquirement of those habits and dispositions, which will qualify us to be made partakers of eternal bliss in another and a better world. If it were possible that he who has made it his first and chief concern to serve and please God, could lose the hope set before him in the Gospel, there is no doubt that he would still consider his choice as a wise one,—that he would consider himself as having gained, on the whole, more happiness than he who made mere worldly objects his primary aim. Still it must be admitted that Christian duty has its trials; and that few comparatively of those who do sincerely endeavour to lead a religious life, would, without the hopes of the Gospel, have acquired that command over their own hearts, which would make those sacrifices in all cases easy, which would in all cases make the road of duty the object of their cheerful choice. The world around presents many objects which promise happiness; and though that promise is often vain, and never fully realized, yet it requires no small degree of firmness to make them relinquished without "one lingering longing look." Present objects, from the very constitution of the human frame, must powerfully affect the mind; and it is not till the disciple of Jesus has, in some good degree, acquired that comprehensiveness of soul, which enables him to keep the eye of faith steadily fixed on things unseen,—that those pleasures and pursuits which have this world as their principal, if not their sole object, cease to attract his desires, cease to obscure that solid happiness, which he might so successfully look for from the complete devotement of his heart to God.

There is an obvious reason why the happy consequences of Christian obedience should only be partially, and not certainly attainable in this life. If enough were here to be acquired to satisfy the mind completely, its attention would be much driven off from that futurity which the Gospel discloses; and that purity and strength of virtue, which are so often produced by looking beyond the world and every thing which it affords, would scarcely have been reached,—certainly not in the degree in which they so often present themselves to our delightful contemplation,—which so much contribute to strengthen the conviction, that all the parts of this great system have been arranged by consummate Wisdom and Goodness.

Still there is enough of present happiness to be derived from faithful endeavours to discharge our duty as Christians, to satisfy us that we are serving the best Master; and, taken in connection with the prospects of the Gospel, to convince one whose understanding is not completely obscured by vicious indulgencies, that the way of duty is wisdom's way. But the present happiness of a virtuous course does not consist in ecstacies and transports; but is, in general, a steady, calm, tranquil, heartfelt satisfaction, which cannot be fully understood, except by those who have felt it. Perhaps the sons of gaiety and pleasure might not regard it as bearing any comparison with the enjoyments which excite their eager desire and ardent pursuit; because it has no quality in common with them; and has even few of those qualities which make those enjoyments for the time so pleasurable. But he who has experienced it will say that their estimate is fallacious; that it is founded in ignorance,—perhaps on a present incapacity to relish those delightful feelings, which spring from the exercise of the noblest affections, and which, when they have lost their vividness by becoming habitual, constitute a source of the purest peace,—peace that surpasses in its value even those joys which the Christian can feel in this imperfect state. It is a peace which passeth understanding. He who hath not at some period of his life experienced it, knows not his loss. And he who has once possessed it, cannot but regard it as his best portion here. If he desert it, to seek any of the pleasures or honours which this world can afford, I have no hesitation in asserting that he has found nothing which he feels can be placed in competition with it,—nothing which, were he free from the slavery of selfish inclinations, he would not gladly give up for it, though that should be what makes the world around look upon him as an object of envy.

The sources of the Christian's peace are obvious. God hath so constituted the human mind, that the faithful discharge of duty is seldom unaccompanied with inward satisfaction. It is that present reward, with which virtue is usually attended, even without any explicit reference to a future life. It is not perhaps so great in the minds of those who have full and extensive ideas of Christian requisitions; and who habitually look beyond the present scene for the consummation of the Christian's happiness. But it is in all cases a freedom from those painful emotions, which the conscience so often produces, where its commands are not obeyed. But there is something beyond and above this. There is a consciousness of the Divine approbation, and a hope of a blessed immortality, which, where they can be indulged with the sanction of the Gospel declarations, afford a peaceful tranquil delight, beyond what language can describe. It is true that the views which we regard as scriptural, respecting the nature of religion, and the tests of religious worth, will not often allow those ecstatic feelings, on which so many of our fellow-Christians rest, as grounds of the conviction that they are the children of God, and possess an interest in the merits of the Redeemer's blood. And he who is in earnest endeavouring to follow the steps of his Great Master, will generally be too sensible to his own deficiencies, to allow of that *confident* expectation, which, where it can be rightly indulged, is enough to absorb the thoughts and affections from temporal objects. But agreeably to those ideas which the Scriptures afford, of the mercy of God, and of the terms of final acceptation, the disciple of Jesus can consistently cherish the humble belief, that his efforts to discharge the duties of life, his exertions to cultivate the spirit of the Gospel and to subdue the dispositions which it forbids, meet with the approbation of Him, who is greater than our hearts, and knoweth all things. He can consistently cherish the humble hope that, through the mercy of God in Jesus Christ, the state of death will be to him a passage to an inheritance incorruptible, undefiled, and unfading. This peace the Gospel presents to all who faithfully endeavour to regulate their hearts and lives by its dictates. It sometimes happens that early habits, or the influence of the bodily constitution of the mind, prevent the enjoyment of those present rewards which would make the religious life what it should be, a cheerful life; and too often the peace which obedience would yield, is chequered by the recollection of past neglects, past transgressions. But, though the Christian may often be unable to mount the commanding eminence from which he might lose the present in the prospect of the future, though his general situation may be in the valley of humility, and that may sometimes be in the vale of tears, yet, mixed with an humbling sense of great unworthiness and much imperfection, he has those delights which spring from the exercise of the best affections, those mild emotions of peaceful satisfaction, which are afforded by the consciousness of more faithful endeavours to comply with the Gospel terms of pardon and acceptance, and those hopes of Divine mercy and approbation, which make humility itself more elevating than the proudest triumphs of the ambitious and worldly mind. The eye may be dimmed by the tear of penitence; but it can still discern the promised inheritance,—it can still discern the hand of a Father, guiding and upholding the wavering step. And even sorrow gradually softens down, till it only affords a slight shade, to make the prospect more suitable to a state of trial and probation.

The sources of Christian peace are, in great measure, independent of the world. The character of it is less turbulent than the pleasures of the world,—more durable and less mixed with the uncertainty which attends the fairest human prospects; and it has no sting concealed, to wound the heart, and make that, which was grasped at as happiness, prove in reality a source of wretchedness. It has, in every point of view, a decided superiority over the pleasures which the world offers; and even over those which the world really affords. It is inconsistent with no pursuit or disposition which has a tendency to promote our real good or that of others. On the contrary, with respect to those pursuits which wisdom points out as our duty or as consistent with our duty, it tends to smooth our difficulties and to sweeten our labours; and, with respect to those dispositions, which the best views of human nature show to be calculated to promote our happiness, it gives aid to the exercise of them, and derives from them materials to increase its own satisfaction. In this period of uncertainty and change (1810) the value of the Christian peace shines pre-eminent. At all times there is a great degree of uncertainty attending the attainment and possession of any earthly good. God hath so ordered the affairs of this world, in connection with the moral state of man, that this is necessary for his improvement in the most valuable qualities necessary to induce him to look beyond what this world affords for his lasting happiness. But at the present time, it is peculiarly striking; and forces itself upon the observation of every one, who has even common experience of life. It seems impossible to calculate with any reasonable security, what may be the worldly situation of any one, when a few months have expired. Our national affairs seem rapidly approaching to a crisis; and what the result may be, God only knows.

Happy they who have learnt to seek their chief happiness in the acquisition of the spirit of the Gospel, rather than in the acquisition of temporal good;—who have learnt rightly to value the objects of time and sense, as designed by our beneficent Creator to excite to the culture of the best dispositions and affections, as designed to sweeten the exertions of life, and to make our journey pleasant through the pilgrimage state; but not to be regarded as our chief good, not to be pursued as the one thing needful, not to be made to engross our best affections and our most earnest exertions; in short, as designed to be pursued and enjoyed with moderation, and under the guidance of Christian principles, and with subordination to the things that are eternal. That they should have their peace unmoved by the uncertainty which hangs over their own earthly prospects, and that of those whom they love, and whose happiness is intimately connected with their own, is in this life not to be expected. It is perhaps impossible that the views should be so enlarged, the comprehension of the mind so extended, as always to consider events in their real tendencies, and thus to rejoice in them, however afflictive they may appear to ourselves or to those whom we love. But those who have regulated their dispositions by the spirit of the Gospel, can in all believe that mercy guides; and, by the exercise of habitual resignation, can check those harassing, corroding, emotions, with which earthly disappointments are long attended, where the heart is not brought into subjection to the obedience of Jesus. And it is in periods of affliction, that the peace of Jesus is seen by all to be of such inestimable value.—Often has it made the bed of sickness, and the approach of death, tranquil and even cheerful. Often has it mixed in the bitter cup of affliction consolations of which the world knows nothing,—which those cannot know whose hearts are not in some good degree moulded by the spirit of Jesus. There are periods when all outward sources of happiness lose their power; and when no human friend can, even by the most affectionate sympathy, afford comfort and support to the drooping heart. Then has the consolation which religion affords often transfused itself; and, in the midst of the thickest darkness, produced a tranquil soothing satisfaction, a peaceful feeling of resignation, and of hope in the Divine mercy; for the loss of which no earthly happiness, however great and permanent, would in any degree compensate.

Before I conclude, I would observe in the First place, that, since the privileges of the Gospel are so great, it becomes us highly to prize it; and to cultivate the highest gratitude to the Father of mercies, to whose love towards man we owe its rich blessings. And when we recollect how much Jesus laboured to afford us those prospects, which, in numberless instances, have enabled his followers to overcome the world, we surely cannot hesitate to offer to him also the tribute of admiring affectionate gratitude. But here we must not rest. Since he spoke and acted under the authority of God, we owe him implicit obedience. This is the honour with which we must honour him, if we honour the Father; and if we slight his authority, we slight the authority of Him who sent him. All we have to do, is to ascertain whether his precepts belong to our own particular cases; and if they do, we are as much bound to obey them, as if God had, by a special messenger from heaven, communicated them to each of us individually.

Secondly:—To possess that peace which the Gospel affords, we must make it our faithful and habitual endeavour, to cultivate the spirit of the Gospel, and to regulate our conduct by its precepts. Half measures will not succeed in religion. Perhaps those who only partially and irregularly endeavour to serve God, are in this life less happy (I do not mean less safe, but less happy,) than those who, without any sense of religion, prudently pursue this world's good. Those who do not live in the fear of God, and are thoughtless of His commands and threatenings, can enjoy temporal pleasures without those pangs of conscience, which attend the unlawful pursuits and pleasures of persons, who have religion enough to show them their danger and folly, but not enough to make them wise unto salvation. Certainly, there is more room to hope, when the conscience is not seared; and therefore the state of such persons is less dangerous. But, I repeat it, to possess the peace which the Gospel affords, we must faithfully give ourselves up to the cultivation of the spirit of the Gospel, and to obedience to its precepts. We must make it our chief aim to serve and please God.

Thirdly, and lastly;—Let me exhort my young friends carefully to shun those pursuits and pleasures, which will embitter their peace; and, above all, carefully to avoid whatever will weaken the religious principles of others, and lead them to depart from the path of God's commandments. He who hath unhappily wandered from the path of Christian peace and uprightness, who hath neglected to cultivate those dispositions which are necessary to the Christian character, may, by timely repentance and reformation, regain the forfeited favour of God; and, though he can never regain that situation in which he would have stood, if he had always endeavoured to live as seeing Him who is invisible, yet he may rightly indulge in the Christian's peace. But, if he have caused others to disobey the holy laws of God, or contributed to lessen the power of right dispositions, his own hopes of pardon will always be alloyed by the distressful reflection, that others are, in part by his means, deprived of it; and his peace will be often disturbed by the consciousness of having contributed to lead others in the broad path of destruction. To possess the Christian's peace, in its purest and most lasting form, requires the early and full devotement of the heart and life to Christian duty.

"There is no peace, saith my God, to the wicked!" And, on the other hand, it is seldom, that, when the mind is sincerely devoted to Christian obedience, it is without a great share of its present rewards. But be that as it may, the time will come when every faithful effort to acquire the dispositions of the Gospel, every honest endeavour to curb the excesses of self-love, every sacrifice of worldly pleasures or interests to the laws of the Gospel, will meet with an ample recompence. The time will come when the dispensations of God will be fully vindicated; and when those who have acted in dutiful submission to His will, shall experience the joyful issue of their privations and exertions, by admission into that state where sin and sorrow shall be known no more for ever.

May those prospects direct our course through the perplexities of life, and support us under all its trials; and may we finally be owned and approved as faithful disciples of Jesus.—Amen.

SERMON XV.

"THE WILL OF THE LORD BE DONE."

ACTS XXI., 14.

THE WILL OF THE LORD BE DONE.

How soothing these words to the friends of Paul! The bare repetition of them seems to dispose the mind for the resigned submission which they manifest.—Whether it be that we have heard them from the venerable lips which breathed the pious sentiment of the heart, or have ourselves been able to employ them in prior seasons of sorrow, they throw a calm over the soul, and prepare it for those consolations, which, when their full influence is experienced, enable us, through the deepest gloom of affliction, to see the hand of mercy, and to acknowledge the dealings of Him, who doth all things wisely and well.

"The will of the Lord be done." Who is without some perception of its tranquillizing influence? May this be experienced by all our friends who now have calls, of various nature, to exercise submission and resignation to the will which is wisest and best; may it be experienced by all of us, when in our turn we are called to bear the chastenings of the Heavenly Parent!

And sooner or later it will be our turn. You will agree with me that, in the brightest scenes of human happiness in this world, (however unmixed with shade when hope points out the future, or memory glances at the past), much really occurs to dim the vividness of fancy's colouring. You will agree with me that suffering and sorrow (either personal or for others,) are so common a portion of the lot of man, that he only can be secure from interruption in his tranquillity, who has learnt to stay his soul upon God; to lay his heart to rest on His will; to consider every affliction and every care as from His hand; to view distress, or pain, or solicitude, as it affects himself personally, as a part of His dicipline; and, in the calamities of others, in the nearer or the wider relations of life, to cherish the conviction that the purposes of them, whether seen or unseen, are such only as Infinite goodness can prompt, and Infinite wisdom direct. I do not mean that, in this state of things, the causes of suffering and solicitude can be *unfelt;* but their *bitterest poignancy* is not known, where the heart has been so trained as true religion can train it. Or if this be for a short time experienced, (as even he experienced it, whom the all-wise Father taught what anguish and darkness are, for the perfecting of his own excellence and for the benefit of those whom he was to lead on to glory,) it is only to give exercise to that submission which bringeth a peace that passeth understanding, while it enables the sufferer to say, "Father not my will but thine be done."

By the merciful appointment of the Father of our spirits, even mental suffering may be alleviated by the recurrence of those trains of thought and feeling, which by degrees turn the attention of the mind from the cause of it, and *for* suffering and *with* suffering, introduce peace; and this in precise proportion to the habitual recurrence of those trains. If we have accustomed ourselves frequently to dwell upon such thoughts and feelings when suggested to us, to seek for them when circumstances in any way call for their influence, to cherish the habits of mind which are in consonance with them, and to check those dispositions and opinions which tend to exclude or to weaken them, they become so habitual as to recur with readiness and almost certainty, in the hour of need.

Among the sentiments which have this supporting tranquillizing influence, you would naturally expect the distressed servant of God to think of Him as the author of all events, and to own His hand even in those which appear most afflictive, to dwell with simple, heartfelt faith on the words of him who is the way, the truth, and the life,—that not a sparrow falleth to the ground without our heavenly Father, and that even the hairs of our heads are all numbered: to call to mind *his* dutiful submission to the will of Him that sent him, when darkness hung over his path, and it was leading through shame and anguish: to rest upon the consideration that the Sovereign Lord of heaven and of earth, is guided in all the works of His hand, and the dealings of His providence, by benevolence unbounded as His wisdom and power; and that he who leadeth us to the throne of God, hath taught us to view this infinitely great and gracious Being as our Father, and to seek at the throne of grace for mercy and for grace to help in time of need.

Not leaving preparation for the trials of life to the periods when all support is needed, contemplation on the circumstances of others, and on the ends of our existence, has often brought into view the purposes and effects of affliction; and the serious thoughtful mind would trace with satisfaction its frequent effects in ameliorating the disposition, in leading the heart to turn its attention upon itself, in teaching it invaluable lessons of humility, in breaking the bondage of evil habits, in preparing it for those of duty, in tutoring the soul for sympathy, in leading to him who hath the words of everlasting life, and who offers rest to the soul, in cherishing that love and confidence towards the Father of mercies which forms so essential a part of spiritual excellence.

In preparing for the hour of need, the disciple of Christ will have dwelt with interesting satisfaction on the manifestations which personal knowledge or faithful biography have presented to his reflection, of trust and resignation, of humble submission, of grateful confidence, of filial faith and duty; and thereby learnt *how* they support, and *what* they have supported. From the present sense of duty, and perhaps looking forward to the hour of trial, he must carefully check those habits and dispositions which oppose the growth of resignation in his own soul; he must aim to lessen that proud self-willedness which is the chief source of human misery; he must give no permanent room to those doubts respecting the dealings of providence, which, whatever foundation they may have in the appearance of things, have none in the reality;—but, on the other hand, he must cherish by all the exercises of faith and piety, and by the considerations presented by the wise and good, the conviction that if all is not clear (and to human knowledge it cannot be,) all is right.

With such culture,—learning habitually to regard affliction not as a punishment (unless indeed brought on by sin or folly), but as chastisement, corrective discipline, directed by the hand of mercy,—all the feelings of tranquil acquiescence would become familiar to him; every exercise of them would render them more easy of introduction; they would recur when they were required, with readiness and almost with certainty; and though they would not annihilate the pang of tenderness, though they would not entirely dissipate the apprehensions of solicitous affection, though they would not stop the flow of those tears which are the tribute of friendship or of sympathy, they would temper the sorrows and solicitudes of humanity, and gradually shed over the soul that holy calm which prepares for duty, which leads to God, and which, even in sorrow, suffering, and care, gives a foretaste of heaven.

There is in our collection a hymn, which so much embodies and expresses the supports of religion in the hour of trial, that under the blessing of God, it has proved of incalculable service to many, very many, who have needed them. I refer to the 431st, derived from the poems of Mrs. C. Richardson, published under the care of Mrs. Cappe. The author is not of our own religious denomination; but the spirit of Christ, the essence of religious faith, is confined to no visible church.

> When sorrow sinks my spirit down,
>   And grief o'erwhelms my troubled mind,
> Faith cries, "Look up to God alone,
>   A refuge thou in Him shalt find."
> My soul obeys the sacred word,
> And casts her care upon the Lord.
>
> What though affliction's shades surround
>   My path, yet God is wise and just;
> And oft my fainting soul has found
>   The promise true, in which I trust:
> Shall I then doubt His sacred word?
> No,—let me humbly trust the Lord.

> 'Tis in the hour of deep distress
>   That we religion's comfort prove;
> The chastening hand we feel and bless
>   Of God, that scourges us in love:
> Though nature sinks beneath the rod,
> Yet faith reposes still in God.

Were any thing needed to render it deeply interesting and edifying, it might be found in the fact, that this hymn was written when the author, then a servant, through unjust aspersions on her character, was thrown on the wide world with no parent or friend to aid her, without the solace of friendship, even without the prospect of a livelihood, in the strictest sense "houseless, sole, forlorn;" and in these circumstances, in the full exercise of trust and duty, she wrote this admirable hymn. It came from the spirit of godliness, and it has often led the spirit to God.

> It is the Lord that strikes the blow,
>   Let every murmuring thought be still:
> Oft has He made my cup o'erflow,
>   And shall I dare dispute His will?
> For ever be the thought abhorr'd;
> My soul! still wait thou on the Lord.
>
> Wait, till He bid thy sorrows cease,
>   Till He thy every care remove;
> And though thy troubles fast increase,
>   Thou need'st not doubt thy Father's love:
> Though He delay, yet trust His word:
> For true and faithful is the Lord.
>
> Yes—Israel's God was never known
>   To leave His children in distress:
> Mercy and truth surround His throne,
>   His judgments all are righteousness:
> Still shall my soul this truth accord;
> I will for ever trust the Lord.

Yes, the resignation of faith and duty enables the weak to support what might to them have seemed insupportable. It brings with it so many tranquillizing considerations, so many elevated sentiments,—all of which tend to lessen the acuteness of suffering and solicitude,—that the mind into which it completely enters, will not sink long under the pressure, however great it may appear.

By a benevolent provision of the Great Being who gave us our spiritual nature, the mind of man, when in a heathful state, seeks involuntarily for that which will lessen the vividness of its painful emotions. At first perhaps it dwells with some sort of satisfaction upon whatever aggravates them; it recalls the past, though the recollection inflicts the severest wounds; but soon with these recollections, others enter, which blend with pain some milder emotions diminishing its acuteness, and preparing the way for the admission of feelings more grateful and more customary to the mind. I do not say that this is the universal progress; but you may often trace it in your own minds, and observe it in others.

But there are sorrows which seem to repel the aid of this natural relief; in which the inroad into the means of happiness is too great to permit its easy reparation. Observe the effects which such causes of affliction produce in minds of different training and dispositions. You see one resorting to the house of festivity, to dissipate the impressions made in house of mourning; you see him drowning his sorrows in noisy gaiety, and endeavouring to drive away feelings which it were good for *him* to indulge, by mixing in the scenes of dissipation, if not of actual sin.

You do not wish to follow his example; nor would I hold up as a pattern the system of him who pronounces it necessary to submit to irresistible fate, declaring it is vain to attempt to remove the burden or to resist it, and that, as it must be borne, it is as well to strive to feel its weight as little as possible;—for though human pride may do much to produce indifference and apathy, these are not qualities of the highest character, nor in general have they any alliance with them.

But observe the man who, from the midst of sorrow, is enabled to bring into view those ideas of the Divine dealings and character, which he has cherished as his soul's best support; see him calmly bowing to the appointment of Providence; see him (in spirit) in the moments of solitude, laying open his sorrows to Him who knoweth every secret of his heart, seeking from Him aid to support them, and grace to sanctify them, and returning from communion with the Father of his spirit, with a heart, not cheerful perhaps, but serene, prepared for dutiful service, and for further trials of faith and patience, grateful for mercies that are past, and in their removal owning His hand, whose love, and mercy, and wisdom, and faithfulness, he has habitually owned and adored. The inexperienced, or those ignorant of religious consolation, may be surprised perhaps to see him thus supported, if they have not observed active courage in his usual deportment, or thought him possessed of that constitutional fortitude which enables him to bear with ease the evils under which others sink; still more, if they have known that he shrinks (if not from suffering in general) from that particular kind of suffering, that he feels acutely, and that he is wounded in the tenderest part. I am convinced you have anticipated me in the cause of his composure; he had fled where all sons of sorrow should fly; and he returned enabled to say, "the will of the Lord be done."

There are few cases in which the cultivation of a right affection is so certainly and readily attended with its reward, as in this of which we are speaking. It is a fact which, were we unable to account for it, we might yet state with perfect confidence, that trustful, dutiful resignation is the most effectual relief under affliction; and that, where it gains complete hold of the mind, it dissipates gloom, though it may not bring light-heartedness, and introduces a holy peace though it may not restore lively cheerfulness.

But were its beneficent effects less obvious, or were any one from a perversion of sentiment to prefer to dwell in gloom, still would resignation be a duty; for in the first place, its elementary affections are essential to the affections of a general piety. It is formed of submission, and trust, and love; and all that nourishes these, in like manner nourishes the sentiments and emotions of resignation. If it be not an inmate in the breast, it is because the corroding influence of self-love and self-consideration have not been sufficiently checked, to allow the best affections of our nature an opportunity for their exercise. If repining discontent be the language of the heart, it must be because it is not sufficiently tutored to trust in the goodness of God, to submit to His appointments, to be grateful to Him for past mercies and for present comforts still continued; it is because the love of God has not yet acquired its due sway within. Further, resignation is intimately connected with the feelings of benevolence. The same wrong biasses of the judgment or the dispositions, which prevent its exercise when affliction presents the occasion, will also lead to view with ill-will, those who have in any way contributed to cause it, as well as those who do not appear ready to give that commiseration, which is sought to supply the deficiency of more valuable alleviations: in short, they cultivate that querulous fretfulness which tends so much to destroy the comfort of the social connections, and, by fixing the mind upon its own narrow concerns and on selfish considerations, checks the attention to the concerns, the comfort, and the welfare of others.

Once more, resignation checks that immoderate sorrow which unfits for the due discharge of the duties of life. I am well aware that resignation does not annihilate sorrow; because it supposes the sources of it to exist. I will add more, it does not stop the tear, it does not stifle the sigh, it does not prevent the throb of anguish; but, in the midst of all, it bows to the will of Him who hath appointed the stroke: and when the first struggles of nature are over, it leads the soul to the source of peace, and enables it to imbibe that peace which is felt in the inmost recesses of the soul, which gradually finds its way among the sources of grief, and by degrees diffuses a general tranquillity within, and permits the spirit, with full and complete accordance of the understanding and the affection, to say, "The will of the Lord be done,"—"All is well."

The Christian's duty is clear, and the pattern for his guidance most encouraging; for Jesus wept at the grave of Lazarus, though he was about to call him to life; and in the near prospect of accumulated suffering, and in the actual experience of what was more intense than the agony of the cross, he said, "If this cup may not pass from me but I drink it, Thy will not mine be done." By us, and by all Thy children, O God, may Thy will be done; and every will that opposes it be humbled and resigned!

Here I will conclude. I had prepared to offer you a few considerations respecting the means by which we may be enabled to exercise this duty, when required by the actual experience of trouble, whether it be in the form of worldly loss, or pain, of sorrow, or of solicitude; but I have already in some measure anticipated them; and I may, at any rate, I feel, leave what I have said to your own reflection.—May the peace of God which passeth all understanding keep your hearts and minds in Christ Jesus.

SERMON XVI.

THE WILL OF GOD THE BEST RULE OF DUTY.

PSALM XXXVII., 31.

THE LAW OF HIS GOD IS IN HIS HEART; NONE OF HIS STEPS SHALL SLIDE.

These words of the pious Psalmist clearly imply two important truths;—in the first place, that the Will of God, considered as the rule of duty, is the most safe and secure guide;—and that an habitual regard to His Will is the best preservative from all moral danger. He who steadily aims to regulate his dispositions, and to guide his conduct, by what he knows of the Will of God, cannot wander far or long from the path of duty. He who makes obedience to the Will of God his prevailing motive, who lives in His fear, and under the habitual influence of the desire to obtain His approbation and shun His displeasure, cannot fall into fatal transgressions or neglect of duty. He will walk uprightly; and he will consequently walk securely. He must be restrained, by the power of this ennobling principle, from all known and wilful transgression; and, in so far as he is under the influence of a single steady aim to do the Will of God, he must proceed in the way of duty with consistency, with firmness, with security, and in general with inward peace and satisfaction.

These truths, though distinct, are nevertheless very intimately connected together. The Will of God may be regarded as the Rule of duty, or as the motive to the performance of duty; but there never, perhaps, was an instance, in which the two views were not united in the actual employment of them. He who honestly makes the Will of God his Rule of conduct, can scarcely avoid perceiving that *it is* his duty to act under the influence of a regard to His Will,—that it is his duty to live as seeing Him who is invisible, and (while he endeavours to guide his conduct and his dispositions by the commands of God,) to make the desire of His approbation, the fear of His displeasure, his direct and habitual motives in the regulation of heart and life. On the other hand, he who is really and habitually influenced by the desire to obey the Divine Will, cannot but be led by that desire to use every means in his power to know what is His Will. If he sincerely and heartily desire to obey God, he will make what he knows of His Will the guide of his life. In short, if the desire to obey the Will of God operates powerfully in the heart, the Will of God will be made the guide of duty. And if the Will of God is sincerely and heartily made the guide of duty, the desire to obey the Will of God must necessarily operate powerfully as a motive. If the law of God really is in the heart, it will guide and it will influence. It will show us our duty and prompt us to pursue it. And, when this is the case, it requires but little experience in life to perceive, that our path will usually be free from perplexities and hindrances, moral dangers will be easily foreseen, temptations will have little power; and, in proportion as the Law of God rules in the heart, our footsteps will not slide,—we shall proceed with steadiness and security in the way of duty,—the testimony of an approving conscience will lighten its difficulties,—and, supported by an humble hope of the approbation of Him to whom all hearts are open, this will afford inward peace, and a cheering prospect of neverending happiness in that state where sin and darkness shall be known no more.

In what farther I shall at present lay before you, I shall not attempt to preserve any marked distinction between the Will of God considered as the Rule of duty, and considered as the motive to action; but I shall have only in view to show that the Will of God is the best guide of conduct. At first sight it really appears unnecessary in any way to attempt to prove this. It seems a self-evident maxim, that the Will of an all-wise and good Being must afford the best guidance to His weak and erring creatures; and it is probable that no consistent and serious believer in the existence of such a Being, can entertain a doubt that, wherever the Divine Will is known, it is our duty to obey it, and that it cannot but be for our interest and happiness to obey it. The state of the case however, is, that in a variety of instances we are left, even with all the aid of Revelation (great and important as it is,) to ascertain the Will of God from the beneficial tendency of actions to others or to ourselves; and, in consequence, many moralists have been led to make this tendency the criterion of virtue and the foundation of duty. Others again, observing that the dictates of their consciences afford them a correct and extensive Rule of duty, consider the conscience as the best moral guide; though most of those would allow the necessity of enlightening the conscience by what is known as the Divine

Will by express Revelation. Others have made virtue consist in living according to nature, or in the agreement of actions and dispositions with the circumstances in which the agent is placed. Various other foundations and rules of duty have been proposed, but those are the most plausible. When we consider the speculations of Philosophers on the subject of moral obligation, and the rule of duty, and observe the great diversity which exists among them as to the *theory* of virtue, we might naturally expect to find great difference in the application of their systems to the practical principles of morality; but where they have been in any considerable degree guided by the morality of the Gospel, it will seldom be found that they differ widely on any essential point. Yet it is not a matter of slight importance what we lay down for ourselves as our fundamental principle of duty; some principles are less extensive, others more accommodating; and our views of duty will usually be found to be clear, extensive, correct, and impressive, in proportion as the principle is so which we employ as our foundation.

I do not wish to go so far as one excellent writer has done, and say that virtue consists in voluntary obedience to the Will of God. Undoubtedly every act of voluntary obedience to the Divine Will, is an act of virtue, but an action may surely be virtuous which does not include an explicit reference to the will of God,—which is not produced by the immediate operation of a regard to His will. I admit that, where the mind is habitually under the influence of a regard to the Divine Will, it will operate directly or indirectly in almost every action, and in almost every instance of the exercise or restraint of the affections; but should we therefore deny the character of *virtuous* to *actions* in themselves right where the motive was also right?—for instance, a strong sense of duty, a disinterested desire to promote the happiness of a fellow-creature? Or should we deny the character of *virtuous* to such *motives* or *dispositions*, though for the time at least there was no direct intention of obedience to the Divine Will, or even any idea at the time in the mind that we were in reality acting agreeably to the will of God? I admit again that the character of the action is greatly heightened, if it not only spring from a sense of duty, and a desire to do good, but also from the belief that it was agreeable to the Divine Will, and the desire to obey it. Indeed it has then reached the highest point of excellence. But I contend that an action is truly virtuous, if it be in itself right (*i. e.* conformable to the Will of God), and springing from a sense of duty, or a desire to do good; and that the motives will be so likewise, in proportion as they are pure,—that is, free from a regard to our own real or supposed good.

The excellent writer to whom I have referred (Pearson in his remarks on Paley) has taken, as a definition of virtue, one which only includes the perfection of virtue. I can think of no higher degree of it, than what he lays down as essential to it,—voluntary obedience to the Divine Will. It was the distinguishing excellence of our Saviour's character, that it was his meat to do the Will of God; and, in so far as his disciples imitate the spirit of their venerated Lord, they will approach that height of excellence, in which the will of God will be our will, and His glory our chief aim. But if we refuse the character of virtue to all actions but those which spring from this ennobling motive, we must not only say that the speculative atheist cannot be in any degree virtuous, however much he may act from a sense of justice, of benevolence, &c.; but must deny the appellation of virtuous to the most worthy, just, generous, or humane, actions of those who, while they believe in the existence and government of an Infinitely wise, powerful, and gracious Being, yet have little, if any, explicit regard to His will. Their virtue is defective both in its extent and in its worth; their characters want that grand quality, which is requisite to complete excellence, which cannot fail to give them stability and purity; but, in so far as they observe the laws of benevolence, truth, uprightness, temperance, &c., from a sense of duty, a desire to do good, or any other motive consistent with the Will of God, their conduct is virtuous, and their motives are virtuous also. The real excellence of Pearson's principles of morality, (which have their foundation laid in religion, in a regard to the Will of God), will be preserved, if we define *virtue* to be the *conformity* of dispositions, and of the actions which result from them, to the Will of God.

And here I must observe, before I proceed, that the views of duty which Revelation unfolds to us, will not allow us to separate actions from their motives, when we speak of them as virtuous. Actions may, in themselves considered, be right; and yet, as far as respects the agent, have no moral character, because they spring from no worthy principles within. They may, as far as respects the agent, be even sinful; because, right in themselves, they spring from sinful motives. For instance, the libertine may afford pecuniary aid to a distressed family, in order to gain the confidence and ruin the happiness of one member of it. On the other hand, right motives cannot make a wrong action right. The agent may not be culpable, since his conduct might be wrong through ignorance only; but though his motives may excuse him in the sight of God, they cannot alter the nature of his conduct. The persecutor may really be influenced by the idea of doing God service; and may suppose that what he does is right. But his actions of persecution are not thereby deprived of their real character; they are wrong; and cannot be made right by any motives whatever. For an action to be entitled to the appellation of virtuous, it must not only be right,—that is, conformable to the Will of God;—but it must spring from right motives,— that is, such as are themselves conformable to the Will of God. On this point it might not be useless to enlarge; but I shall at present proceed to observe,—

First:—That by making the Will of God the criterion of virtue, in other words our Rule of duty, we do in fact include every other criterion of virtue, or rule of duty, that is itself reasonable and just. If it is urged, (for instance) that the dictates of conscience should be our Rule of duty, we say that, from attentive consideration of the nature of man, as well as from the declarations of Revelation, it is clear that the conscience was intended by the great author of our frame to be our guide in all cases of emergency, and to have great influence in every department of duty: but that, without due care and culture, it may become, and often is, erroneous and defective;—that therefore it is not safe as an exclusive guide of duty, but should itself be put under the direction of the still higher principle, the Will of God;—that we should enlighten the conscience by the law of God, and other intimations of His Will, and then submit implicitly to its direction; but that it is only where it does direct us in conformity to the Will of God, that it is our duty to obey it. The will of God, therefore, is at last the point to which we must come, if we would judge how far the dictates of conscience ought to govern us. And, though these do of themselves often afford much light as to the Will of God,—though they may sometimes be our only direct guide as to the conduct which will be acceptable to Him,— and in all cases should receive great attention,—yet it is only so far as we have reason to believe the conscience to be conformable to the will of God, that obedience to it is our duty; and the will of God should therefore be our chief guide of duty, and should be employed to regulate, correct, refine, and extend, the dictates of every subordinate principle.

Suppose, again, that the beneficial tendency, or utility, of actions and dispositions, be made the Rule of duty, we reply that, in so far as they really have this beneficial tendency, they must be conformable to the Will of God; and that therefore this rule is also included under the Rule which should be employed as our grand and invariable guide. The beneficial tendency of actions and dispositions, may sometimes be our only guide as to the Will of God; and may often aid us in the application of the Scripture precepts of duty; and still more frequently may serve to show us the grounds and reasons of those precepts, their importance, and subserviency to the welfare of mankind. But the supposed tendency of actions can never be put against the Law of God, as declared to us by Revelation; and should not, therefore, be made our chief rule. The same may be shown of every other criterion of virtue or rule of duty; so far as it is self-consistent, consistent with other principles of duty, and really just and useful, it cannot fail to be included under that one, which it is alike our wisdom and duty to make our invariable guide,—the Will of God. That by which all other principles of duty must be tested, should itself be employed as our constant standard of right and wrong; and this leads me to observe,

Secondly :—That this Rule of Duty is *absolutely universal*; it extends to every part of the external conduct, and to every internal disposition. Some rules of duty leave out of sight important branches of moral excellence; for example, if virtue be made to consist, as some moralists define it, in doing good to others, in benevolent endeavours to promote the welfare of mankind, those important classes of duties which respect piety towards God, and the regulation of our own desires and affections, are completely left out of sight. And I have no doubt, that this deficiency has, in a vast variety of instances, tended to weaken the sense of their obligation, to make them but little thought of, or, if thought of, viewed as not essential to human virtue. When the Will of God is made the Rule of duty, there can be no such deficiency. His Will cannot but respect all our actions, desires, affections, and dispositions. The Laws of God, (by which I particularly understand the Revealed declarations of His Will)—the Laws of God clearly extend to all these; and the attentive observance of the course of Providence, of the dictates of conscience, and of the frame of man, while they aid us in the application of the Divine command, do also serve to show us His Will, in a degree, and with a force, proportioned to the extent and accuracy of our observations. And even if there be any cases in which the Laws of God fail of application, yet, from those sources, the mind sincerely desirous of knowing and doing the Will of God, can seldom be at a loss to discover what it really is.

Again, *Thirdly*:—The Will of God, considered as the Rule of duty, is an *invariable* principle. As far as we are left to ascertain the Will of God from inferior and subordinate rules, this rule must in some measure partake of that uncertainty. But, with the Revealed will of God to aid us, to be a lamp unto our feet and a light unto our paths, to prevent confined experience and erroneous conscience from misleading us, it is extremely seldom that there can be any difference of opinion as to duty, where the Will of God is honestly employed as a standard. If utility be made the criterion of virtue or rule of duty, greater or less degrees of experience, greater or less freedom from the perverting influence of selfish feelings, will lead to widely different convictions,—if not with respect to the justness of the grand principles of duty,—at least with respect to the extent and application of them. If the dictates of conscience (unless it be trained by the very Rule of which we are speaking) be fixed upon as the guide of duty, we shall find them varying in extent, in correctness, and in power, through the influence of fashion, of prejudice, of ignorance, and of prevalent opinions and examples. But he who sets out with the Will of God as his Rule of duty, has a fixed principle, which will not bend to the reasonings of the philosopher, to the opinions of the multitude, or to the promptings of passion. If, indeed, we do not seek for that as the primary principle of duty, we may sometimes be led to fancy that conduct is directed by the Will of God, which is really inconsistent with it. But the more we seek for the guidance of that principle, humbly, sincerely, and earnestly, the more we shall find it; and the more we find it, the more firm, steady, and invariable, must our views of duty become; for the Will of God itself must be invariable.

And here I would observe, *Fourthly:*—That, by taking the Will of God as our Rule of duty, our ideas of duty will gradually become clear, and expansive; and this to a degree which cannot be generally, at least, expected where we rest in any subordinate rules. "Voluntary obedience to the Will of God" has an exalting and expanding influence on the mind. If our own welfare be regarded as the foundation of duty, in so far as we made it our rule, our views would be confined to our own little sphere; we should judge of actions and dispositions, only, or principally, in the relation they bear to personal happiness; and, leaving out of view the intricacies and perplexities in which we should be continually involved, our notions of duty (unless still guided by the rule of Revelation) would be as narrow and contracted as the principle on which they are founded. The same things may be observed, though to a less extent, as to rules of duty founded upon utility and conscience; unless still further guided by the rule of Revelation. So far from expanding as we proceed, our views would usually become limited by difficulties and objections, which, in the commencement of our moral investigation, we had overlooked. But fix upon the Will of God as the Rule of duty, with an impressive conviction on the mind that His Will must be right and good;—we see more and more clearly the tendency of obedience to promote the welfare of His rational creatures;—one moral truth serves as the basis of another;—as we advance, difficulties lessen;—we see things more as they would be viewed by us, if we could take the rule into account, and forget their relations to ourselves; and we learn to view duty in its whole extent, where other rules would leave deficiencies,—we learn to view actions and dispositions without that undue reference to their immediate consequences, to which the subordinate rules of duty must too generally confine us.

This leads me to observe *Fifthly*:—That the Will of God, considered as a Rule of duty, is, in an eminent degree, *a safe guide.* Several eminent moralists, and particularly Paley, have made general expediency the criterion of virtue; and the author of Political Justice (whose moral speculations, though in some cases interesting and valuable, often show the folly of leaving the Will of God as our best guide,) maintains that morality "is nothing but a calculation of consequences, and an adoption of that mode of conduct, which, upon the most comprehensive view, appears to be attended with a balance of general pleasure and happiness."—But it is clear that beings, who cannot see the consequences of any action in their full extent and connections, cannot be adequate judges of general expediency; and that, if they take this as more than a subordinate rule of duty, they must be continually misled by their ignorance and selfish prejudices. The true plan undoubtedly is, to ascertain, as far as we can, what is our duty, taking the Will of God as our Rule and Guide; and then to pursue it, without thinking too much on the particular consequences of our observance of it. "The happiness of the world," Bishop Butler admirably observes, "is the considering of Him who is the Lord and proprietor of it; nor do we know what we are about, when we endeavour to promote the good of mankind, in any ways but those which He has directed."

Sixthly :—The Will of God, considered as a Rule of duty, is a rule which carries with it its own obligation.—It may indeed be said, that there is one ground of obligation beyond it, which is brought into view by that definition of virtue which makes it consist in its tendency to promote the ultimate happiness of the agent. And it is to be allowed, that we may ask, with reverence, why should we obey the Will of God? But the answer is plain and obvious,—because under the government of an Infinitely wise, good, and powerful Being, obedience to His Will must secure our highest welfare. When once asked, it is a question which never need be asked again. Its answer is a self-evident and necessary truth. I say, therefore, that our rule carries its own authority along with it. We cannot think of any higher obligation, than the commands of that gracious Being, under whose government we live, and upon whom we depend now and for ever. We have nothing to do but to know what His will is, and then obey, with full security that we are doing what is wise and right, what in fact is best for others and for ourselves. And it may be observed that, if we make the tendency of actions and dispositions towards our own ultimate happiness, the criterion of virtue, we have no more sure and general guide as to that tendency, than the Will of Him upon whom our ultimate happiness depends; so that, take whatever view of it we will, we come to the same conviction.

Several other reflections occur to the mind, in connection with this subject; but I have already encroached too much upon your time, and I shall for the present only observe—

In the *Seventh* and last place :—That the employment

of the Will of God as our Rule of duty, must almost necessarily lead us to make the Will of God our motive as well as our guide. It is indeed a supposable case, that a person shall habitually employ the exalted rule only for its being the best for him, as the best guide to his highest interests. But such is the constitution of the human mind, that it is scarcely a possible case.—We are so formed, that what we pursue as a means by degrees will become our end. In whatever way we learn the Will of God, (whether by the course of His Providence, by our consciences, by the frame of man, or above all by Revelation,) if we steadily employ it as our Rule and Guide (although in the first instance, because it is our wisdom to do so,—because thus we shall best promote our own welfare,) it must, as we proceed, be continually obeyed without any explicit reference to its consequences to ourselves; and, in proportion to the frequency and constancy of voluntary obedience to the Will of God, it will of itself become our object, our first and chief object. Besides, if we take the Will of God as the guide of duty, it cannot fail to teach us (what other rules too often leave out of sight), that it is our duty to cultivate the disposition to obey Him, to seek for His approbation, to shun His displeasure, to fear Him, to love Him, to trust in Him, and to serve Him; and we cannot therefore doubt, both from the natural tendency of the mind, and from those views of duty which the Will of God communicates, that, if we do make it our guide, we shall necessarily be led to make it our motive. Habitual, universal, voluntary, intentional, obedience to the Will of God, must be the highest point of excellence among all His rational creatures. This motive must carry along with it worth and happiness, security and peace, in proportion to the steadiness and extent of its influence. This, the frame of man and the course of Providence,—this, the light of Revelation,—most expressly and forcibly teach us. In proportion as the Will of God becomes our motive, shall we see clearly, and discharge steadily the whole of our duty. In that proportion shall we become like him, whose grand end and aim was to promote the glory of the Great Being who sent him, and to finish His work. In that proportion shall we become partakers of the Divine nature, and the Will of God become our will.

May it become the language of our thoughts and words and actions, as well as of our direct supplications, —Heavenly Father, may Thy Kingdom come, may Thy will be done on earth as it is done in Heaven.

www.ingramcontent.com/pod-product-compliance
Lightning Source LLC
Chambersburg PA
CBHW021829230426
43669CB00008B/916